Teaching a Young Child to Read

Teaching
a Young Child
to Read

by

Wood Smethurst, Ed.D.

BB
Brookline Books

ISBN 1-57129-048-6

Library of Congress Cataloging-In-Publication Data
Smethurst, Wood.
    Teaching a young child to read / by Wood Smethurst.
       p.   cm.
    ISBN 1-57129-048-6 (pbk.)
    1. Reading (Early childhood) 2. Reading--Parent participation.
  3. Reading--Phonetic method. I. Title.
LB1139.5.R43S64   1998
372.4--DC21   98-12634
                                      CIP

Book design and typography by Erica L. Schultz.

Printed in USA
10 9 8 7 6 5 4 3 2 1

Published by
BROOKLINE BOOKS
P.O. Box 1047
Cambridge, Massachusetts 02238
Order toll-free: 1-800-666-BOOK

❦ Contents

This book is dedicated to my sons,
Frank and William Smethurst,
who were among my first and best pupils,

and to my great mentor,
Professor Jeanne Chall of Harvard University,
who over her distinguished career
has shown us all what teaching is really about.

❦ *Foreword*

Wood Smethurst—teacher, college professor, researcher and head-master—has written a remarkable book to help parents teach their children to read. The book takes the child from pre-reading to accurate reading with comprehension and enjoyment. It includes instruction in phonics, language enrichment, and the reading of literature. Appropriate for children who are first learning to read, it can also be used for older children who are having difficulty.

The reading methods in this book are based on the best available research evidence and on the author's long, successful experience with children. The activities presented will capture the attention and interest of children and parents.

Smethurst also passes along sage advice to parents—to be patient, not to lose their humor, not to press too hard, and not to become too emotionally involved. This book is practical, highly readable, and above all, full of wisdom.

—Jeanne S. Chall, Ph.D.
Professor Emeritus of Reading,
Harvard Graduate School of Education

INTRODUCTION

Helping a Child Learn to Read Well

In my 37 years of teaching, I have spent many memorable hours helping students learn how to read, and among the best and most productive times have been the hours I have been spent helping parents teach their own children to read.

In this book, I will show you how to help your student develop into a good and lifelong reader—starting with prereading skills and building to the point when he or she can read reasonably independently in children's materials, with good understanding and appreciation. This program of phonics, comprehension, and language development is compatible with all preschool and first-grade reading approaches, and is also adaptable for remedial instruction with somewhat older children.

If appropriately taught, nearly all youngsters can learn to read and write. The acquisition of reading and writing skills liberates a child from exclusive dependency on the spoken word, and opens up a world of adult communication that we tend to take for granted. Most children eventually learn to read, but not all learn in the same ways, or with the same facility. First-grade students are often categorized into three groups according to their ease of reading acquisition; let us fancifully call these groups Bluebirds, Robins, and Sparrows. About a third of youngsters, the Bluebirds, seem to learn to read well no matter what kind of instruction they receive or what materials they use. Another third, the Robins, appear to learn well enough, but differences in materials and instruction are reflected in their achievement. The final third, the Sparrows, learn to read slowly and with considerable difficulty. Individually tailored instruction will be needed for these children to learn to read well.

Research and practice both suggest that the best overall approach is one that combines a strong and varied whole-language experience with lots of phonics (Durkin, 1974). The controversy between phonics and whole language is, I believe, unfortunate: children need both types of instruction. This program teaches essential concepts and skills of phonics and language comprehension in an easygoing and low-key manner.

Some background is appropriate here. A review of home and school reading instruction over the past several centuries suggests that early beginnings in the home are quite helpful, and that the more a child knows about reading when she begins school, the better. Children who enter first grade with some reading skills— such as knowledge of letter names, words, and sounds—are likely to succeed in first-grade reading instruction (see Chall, 1967; Durkin, 1974; Durrell, 1964; Manguel, 1996; Smethurst, 1975, 1987).

It is worthwhile to reflect on how reading develops—from its earliest beginnings in language acquisition and readiness, through phonics and word recognition, into fluent reading and mature comprehension, appreciation, and analysis. Even though learning to read is sometimes spotty and is occasionally difficult, especially for some children, there is still something of an orderly progression in this learning process. Children learn to read in many ways, but they generally pass through certain way stations along their journey:

1. *Readiness, or Emergent Literacy.* The child learns to speak and respond to spoken language, learns basic concepts underlying reading and written language, and may learn letter names and some sounds.

2. *Beginning Reading.* The child learns letters, sounds, and some sight words, and learns to read simple sentences (e.g.,

The fat cat sat, or *This is Spot.*).

3. *Word Recognition.* The child learns to recognize more and more words by sight and by using phonics skills. Phonics, syllabication, and common sight words are taught.

4. *Fluency and Automatization.* The child learns to read with more and more fluency and expressiveness, and begins to incorporate automatic word recognition processes into his reading.

5. *Reading for Interest.* The child begins to read more widely, often pursuing interests in a variety of subjects. This extensive reading leads the student to develop greater fluency and understanding.

6. *Mature Reading.* The student reads well, with fluency and good understanding, in a variety of materials.

Those interested in learning more about these stages are encouraged to read Jeanne Chall's seminal *Toward a Stage Theory of Reading.**

Making Sure the Child Becomes a Good Reader

You can make certain a child learns all the concepts and skills necessary for capable reading, regardless of what his school does or doesn't teach. The study program in this book supplements in-school reading instruction, which research and experience have often shown to be incomplete for some children; early-grade teachers are often so busy that they cannot provide *all* the practice in phonics or the language enrichment that a particular child may need. The following chapters describe, in a carefully laid-out sequence of steps, what you can do to help a child learn to read—and, we hope, to enjoy reading as well.

---

* Readers who want to know more about phonological awareness and the concepts underlying children's beginning to read are encouraged to see Marilyn Adams' important book, Beginning to Read (MIT Press: 1994). Increasingly, researchers are coming to believe that difficulty with these understandings underlie many reading and learning problems.

THE PROGRAM

So far we have considered several theoretical aspects of teaching young children to read. The rest of this book will focus on actual reading instruction. In the following pages I suggest what you can do to teach a child to read, as well as when and where you should do it. In addition to my own guidelines, I will suggest several published reading programs for those who want to use a highly structured approach. However, I suggest these only as supplements to reading together, writing, playing games, creating scrapbooks and journals, and so on. No published program can or should take the place of these other activities.

General Information

A striking fact about young readers is that they have often been read to regularly by parents, sitters, siblings, or someone else; in ideal circumstances, they also sit so that they can see the pictures and words of the books being read. Other common factors in the homes of early readers include the presence of lots of books, especially children's books, and the presence of people who value books and value reading. In addition, since early readers are often also early scribblers, these children usually have access to an abundance of writing materials—paper, crayons, pencils, markers, chalkboard and chalk, and maybe even a typewriter or computer. Many early readers are also TV fans. It is interesting to speculate about the number of readers who have been inspired by *Sesame Street*.

It may help to say something here about the rate at which children progress in reading—especially when you begin with a very young child. Children two to three years old often seem to learn in fits and starts, to be sponges one time and sieves the next. Don't worry. Take it as it comes. If you're interested in the letters, the child will be interested too, and sooner or later she'll learn them. Of all the phases of learning to read, learning the letters takes the longest, sometimes a year or more (although it is not uncommon to hear of children who learned their letters in a day or two when they really got involved). The best thing that can be said of the task is that children learn at their own speeds and in their own ways. It is usually folly to measure one child against another, so please don't try.

As you begin to teach a child about reading, it is important to ease into the process slowly. Recognize that the largest step any child will make in learning to read is understanding three fundamental concepts:

1. What is spoken can be written (and vice versa).
2. Print stands for speech.
3. Reading is useful and pleasant.

In my view, if the child understands these ideas, you're well on your way. I consider these three factors to be the essence of reading readiness. Paradoxically, you can begin reading aloud, playing language games, writing, and playing with letters very early—indeed, many parents now begin these activities with their children in infancy.

Specific Suggestions

There are several specific suggestions that will hold regardless of the teaching program you decide to follow and the general circumstances of your instruction.

1. Try to read to your pupil at least 20 minutes every day, in pleasant circumstances, and make sure that she can see the words and pictures as you read. Choose reading material that your student wants to read. Ideally, the two of you should make a big occasion of selecting and comparing books together—either at the library, at the bookstore, or on the Internet.

2. Try to arrange for the child to watch *Sesame Street*. This widely acclaimed program is grounded in the same research base as the method outlined here, and should make your task easier. I have reservations about a lot of TV watching in

the life of any child—especially after age 6 or so—but a moderate amount can be helpful. (I consider up to an hour a day to be moderate.)

3. Encourage your student to draw, scribble, and write. Have chalk and a chalkboard, paper, markers, pencils, and a computer available in your student's room or another place where they can be reached easily.

4. Play games involving basic reading skills—knowledge of letter names, letter sounds, words, and so forth. (Specific games will be described in the kits.)

5. Purchase a set of magnetic letters for the refrigerator door and start to use them.

6. Try to find inexpensive paperback children's books matched with tapes of actors reading the books (these are put out by the Scholastic Press and various other children's publishers). Using a tape, the child can look at the book and hear it read at the same time. If you have a children's tape player, the child can play the tapes and read the books unassisted. This is sometimes a nice solution for busy parents. CD's and videotapes that do much the same thing are also available.

7. Surround your student with books, newspapers, posters, and magazines. If you have a computer, let her use it under supervision.

8. Make written language important around your house or classroom. Call attention to the times when you need to read, and comment on how great it is to be able to read.

9. Point out words and letters on signs, billboards, TV shows, labels, headlines, posters, etc.

10. Show your pupil how to write his name, your name, and the names of friends, pets, relatives, and others.

11. Together with your student, make frequent trips to libraries,

magazine racks, and/or bookstores, and shop the Internet. Get some books and magazines for *both* of you. Your student should see you reading, too, because your actions speak very loudly. Make it clear that you value reading and read books both for information and for pleasure. Read often.

12. Relax—don't push. *Never work on reading unless your student wants to, and always quit when your student wants to quit* (it is preferable to quit *before* the child wants to).

13. Keep your anxiety for the child to be "right" out of your voice. If you show him *X* and he says *Y*, don't become tense or impatient. Children learn, but it takes time. Learn from mistakes—figure out why he confuses *X* with *Y*, and then try to clear up the confusion. This easy acceptance is at the heart of teaching, and it should be very satisfying to both of you.

14. Follow the program outlined in Chapter 5, or if you purchase one of the commercially available programs* for teaching young children, continue to supplement it with the language activities outlined in this book.

15. Never use emotional pressure of any sort to get your student to learn to read. Never work on reading when the child does not want to work. Make reading a fun interlude that he asks for. Try to build it into his daily schedule (e.g., reading to him each night before he goes to bed). Again, remember to stop when the child wants to stop—preferably *before* he wants to stop—and *never push him to read. Keep it a game.*

---

* Though it is quite difficult for inexperienced teachers because of its unusual format, one of the best teaching materials is the Programmed Reading Series by Sullivan Associates, published by Phoenix Press (1971). (Even the *Whole Earth Catalog* recommended it for teaching reading in the commune, or whatever.) Also useful is Dolores Durkin's text *Teaching Them to Read* (1974), which provides many ideas and activities for kindergarten or primary teaching that can also be used in the home.

The Kits

The program outlined in the remainder of this book was developed over the past 30 years, during which time I have been a parent, a preschool and elementary school teacher, a graduate student at Emory and Harvard, a reading specialist, a college professor, the director of the Emory University Reading Center, and the Headmaster of Ben Franklin Academy and its associated learning clinic. This reading program takes the form of 27 "kits"—lessons for parents, teachers, or other tutors to use with young children on an individual basis. It is specifically designed with children under age 7 in mind, to appeal to their inherent curiosity, playfulness, and desire to learn.

I hope this program will work for you. I have attempted to distill the best and most effective combination of all the methods and materials available. In each kit, I provide thorough descriptions of all the games and materials involved. I have concentrated on using inexpensive, easy-to-find, homemade materials; you do not have to be wealthy to teach your child.

The Readiness section of this program, consisting of Kits 1-4, describes the program elements in great detail. Directions are provided for such activities as reading aloud, writing, constructing reading-related projects, learning from mail, e-mail, and various other forms of media, playing learning games, and selecting appropriate reading materials.

In the sections that follow Readiness, the basic instructions will not be repeated. Teachers and parents whose children already know letters and sounds, and who want to start at Kit 5, are urged to read over Kits 1-4 anyway. Much of the teaching advice given in those kits is applicable throughout the program.

Before going into any further details, it is important to clarify what this program is *not*. This program is not

1. *Automatic*. You'll have to work at it.

2. *Infallible*. Some children don't learn to read easily with any method, including this one.

3. *A complete first-grade-to-high-school reading course.* This book leaves off at about the point where the child can read children's books and other materials independently—which translates to a second- or third-grade reading level.

4. *Meant for high-pressure teaching.* If you want to push a child, get another program—or, better yet, push some area less sensitive than reading, like table manners, tooth brushing, or cleaning up one's room.

Teaching a child to read can be one of the most satisfying experiences you will ever have. There is only one major *don't: Don't get anxious and start to apply pressure.* Once you do that, the process is no longer a game for the child, and therefore is no longer fun. It becomes a matter of working to please an adult, which is the antithesis of the kind of learning that this program seeks. Once you start to pressure a child, or to fret over how much or how little progress is being made, you have failed.

TROUBLESHOOTING

If at any time your student doesn't seem to understand the ideas you are trying to teach, back off and try to figure out why. Don't be anxious. After all, there's plenty of time.

The first question to ask yourself is "Am I pushing too hard?" Another question to ask is "How did this child go about learning the previous material?" Try to figure out if she seems to learn in some distinctive way.

If you find you're still not getting anywhere, take a week off. Do the especially fun things, but hold the instruction for a while; just enjoy written language together. For that week, don't even try to teach whatever it is that's not getting across. Concentrate on reading aloud together, writing stories, searching the Internet, or keeping a journal. Then, after you've been away from the instructional material for a while, see if you can come back for a fresh start and a fresh approach.

Some children, especially those with learning disabilities, have very serious difficulties in learning to read. If your student seems unable to go beyond a certain point, stop trying to teach him to read, and concentrate on reading and writing *with* him. Whatever you do, don't push; applying pressure can cause many problems, emotional and otherwise, for both of you.

Don't be afraid to depart from this program at any point to try your own ideas. Any game you invent is likely to work better than mine: because it comes from you, your pupil will probably enjoy it. If you have any questions about what to do, or about whether or not a particular method is appropriate, please write to me at the following address:

Dr. Wood Smethurst
Ben Franklin Academy
1585 Clifton Road
Atlanta, Georgia 30329

Also visit our Web page (http://www.mindspring.com/benfrank) and read the special section on early reading. I welcome your e-mail—my address is benfrank@mindspring.com.

This is my project, and I enjoy talking about it. I would also greatly appreciate hearing about games you think up so I can share them with other parents. Any ideas, changes, and additions you suggest will be more than welcome. Enjoy.

UNIT I

Readiness: Kits 1-4

This unit provides natural ways you can develop your student's reading readiness, helping him to learn basic concepts, letter names, and letter-sound associations, and to recognize a few words by sight. Emphasis is placed on reading and writing for meaning.

🐝 *Kit 1: The capital letter names*

MATERIALS

- Capital letter poster (homemade)
- Capital letter cards (3 x 5" index cards lettered by felt-tip pen)
- ABC books and other children's books (from the library or bookstore)
- Child's chalkboard and chalk
- Typewriter or word processor
- Personal computer or Web TV

GOALS

The point of this kit is to help your student become interested in reading and in learning the names of the capital letters—just the names for now. You needn't bother with their sounds, alphabetical order, or lower-case forms just yet. We'll get to those in due time with later kits.

When your pupil can name all the capital letters, in any order that you point to them, you are ready for Kit 2.

INSTRUCTIONS

1. What to do

This section provides a broad summary of Kit 1; the following sections treat the individual steps in detail. With steps *(a)* and *(b)* you will try to get the child interested in reading; with steps *(c)* through *(h)* you will try to get her interested in letters and written language.

    a. You and your student should be reading together on a regular basis. If you are not doing so already, this is *the* place to start.

b. Now is also a good time to add to the child's book collection. Take trips to the library or bookstore, and browse Internet book sources and catalogues.

c. Make a poster or letter strip of the capital letters for the child's bedroom, playroom, or classroom (or make several posters and letter strips). Also make capital letter cards, using 3 x 5" index cards and felt-tip pens. Try to find plastic letters and a child's chalkboard in your local toy store, or order them by mail. Keep writing materials (and, if possible, a computer) available to your student. Encourage the child to try to write for herself.

d. In capital letters, print the child's name—as well as any other words he'd like to see—on a card, piece of paper, or chalkboard.

e. Play letter learning games together.

f. Watch *Sesame Street* together.

g. Write stories together—make them up by yourself or in collaboration with your student, or have her dictate them for you to transcribe.

h. Use the written language all around you—on TV, signs, advertisements, labels, headlines, etc.—to call attention to different letters and words.

If you and your student are already accustomed to talking about letters, by all means keep it up. If you are not, this is a good time to start. Around the house or classroom, on trips or walks together, or whenever else you think of it, point out letters to your pupil as matters of some interest. With my own children, I recall making observations like the following:

> "This is an *S*—see, it's got a wavy crooked shape like a *sss*snake. It's the letter *S*."

This may seem somewhat silly and undignified to you, but I believe that teachers of small children are well advised to be a little silly and undignified sometimes. This is one of the things that can make teaching a young child so much fun.

As soon as your student knows the names of all the capital letters, start on Kit 2—even if you haven't completed all the activities in Kit 1.

2. Things for you to make or buy

a. *Capital letter poster.* Make a capital letter poster for your student, using a large sheet of paper, several standard-size sheets of paper, or a large piece of posterboard. Write on the poster with a favorite color of felt-tip pen. (If you and the child have no special color preference, blue is good choice, because it stands out and is attractive. I also like red, although there are forms of color blindness that make red harder to see for some children.) While a number of letter posters are commercially available, I like homemade ones better—they're *you,* and they indicate to your pupil that she and the letters are really important to you. Figures 1 and 2 show several possible poster formats.

The poster can be hung on a wall, on the refrigerator, on a door, or in any other location of your choosing. I prefer hanging the poster in the child's bedroom or playroom—I really like the idea of a child being able to see the letters from her bed—but this is hardly necessary; do what you like. You might want to make a poster for the child care center, the kitchen, or another room, and use a letter strip in the bedroom.

Figure 3 gives a chart of directions for printing the capital letters. This program uses simplified manuscript printing, similar to that found in most kindergarten and primary school language arts programs. You may find the numbers and arrows arbitrary, and inconsistent with the way you print one or more of the letters. Feel free to stick to your method of

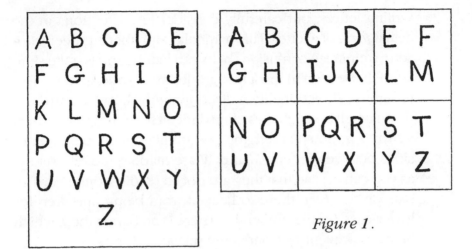

Figure 1.

Figure 2.

Figure 3.

writing letters, but carefully consider any variations in the actual *form* of a letter. This particular alphabet has been chosen to minimize confusions between letters, and is quite similar to those used in most first grades and kindergartens. Determining directionality—discriminating between up and down or left and right—is often difficult for youngsters, which is why I go to such lengths to minimize directional confusions between letters. *M* and *W* are made quite differently, as you can see, so that they are not so readily confused. The bars on the *I* are there to keep it from being mistaken for lower-case *l* or the numeral 1. There is no bar on the *J*, which helps to prevent *J*'s from being mistaken for *I*'s.

Encourage your student to try to recognize her name in capital letters and to write it in capital letters. Print it for her, using large capital letters of the same form you used on the poster. Other possibilities include having her form her name with plastic letters, or having her try to type it (set the computer or typewriter on all caps, and hope for the best). Once your student knows how to spell her name, learning to write it is largely a matter of time.

b. *Capital letters wall strip.* You might want to make a letter strip for the top of your student's bedroom wall (or some other wall). This is especially useful if space is a problem. Any opaque white rolled paper will do—wide adding-machine paper, or even used computer printout paper, is fine.

Using a felt-tip pen, print the letters in a bright color (I prefer blue), as large as you can—2 to 4 inches is a reasonable size range. In use, the strip might look as in Figure 4. I believe a letter strip is best placed so that all the letters are easily visible from the child's bed. I know that this suggestion gets me perilously close to the Puritan ideal of "improving each moment," but a letter strip that your child can see from his bed will get a lot of attention before and after naps and in the early morning. It is also one more item to talk about at naptime or bedtime.

Figure 4.

---

c. *Plastic letters.* Sets of small (1½ x 1½") plastic letters can be bought in many toy and department stores, or by mail order. (You will need lower-case plastic letters for Kit 2, so save yourself trouble by purchasing capital and lower-case letters at the same time.) If you do purchase plastic letters, buy the magnetized ones. These can go on the refrigerator, washing machine, or any other receptive surface, and are excellent tools for working with your student at odd moments.

d. *Capital letter cards.* You can make the letter cards for Kit 1 using 3 x 5" index cards, a black felt-tip pen, and a blue ballpoint pen. Simply print capital letters in black on the cards, one to a card. Draw a blue line across the bottom of each card to help your student remember which side is up (this is much more important with lower-case letters). Try to be reasonably consistent in size, and remember to use the unlined side of the card. Follow the same simplified alphabet as used on the poster (see Figure 5, p. 22).

e. *Chalkboard and chalk.* These should be easily found in stores near you. If not, they may be ordered by mail. A discussion of how your student's natural interest in writing can help him learn to read is found in Section 5 of this kit.

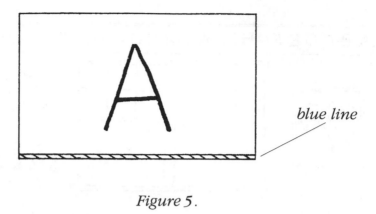

Figure 5.

---

   f. ABC blocks. You might also want to purchase ABC blocks.
   These are usually not expensive, and have been a standby
   for many years. In general, the more items with the letters
   on them your student sees, the easier it will be for her to
   learn the letter names.

3. Reading aloud

You should be reading to your student for at least 20 minutes daily—
twice that, if possible. Be sure that you make reading together a
warm, pleasant, and relaxed experience, easy and fun for both of
you. Sit close together so the child can see the pages as you read,
and point out "where it says *Mickey*" or anything else you think will
be of interest in the text. Don't overdo this, though; keep it light
and fun.

   Don't ever let reading get to be a bore. *Only read to the child
when he wants you to, and always try to stop before he loses interest.* Keep it fun.

4. Books & magazines

This program relies on developing a familiarity with books, stories,
poems, and other forms of written language. A good way to begin
is by starting a collection of children's books. Large, colorfully illustrated books are most likely to get your student's attention and ap-

proval. Many of these books are available at libraries, and can be purchased inexpensively in paperback editions. Also watch out for book fairs and used book sales.

Only you and your student can determine what sorts of books you will enjoy. I have some difficulty with graded book lists, since young children often seem able to understand and enjoy books with relatively advanced phrasing and formats, especially when these are read *to* them. I recommend Nancy Larrick's classic book *A Parent's Guide to Children's Reading* (1975, revised in 1979), which provides good advice and background for making these decisions.

It is a good idea to take your student to the library and make a considerable to-do over the selection of books to read together. This is, after all, an important matter, and it deserves careful consideration from both of you. With luck, you'll be able to find a librarian who has a good knowledge of children's books and is interested in helping you find the ultimate book. Be sure to keep your student at the center of this book finding. (Many libraries have children's card catalogues or special children's computer programs.) Have your student carry her books home, keep track of them (with some help, perhaps), and return them—emphasizing that she is an important part of this whole reading business.

The prices of books seem to be going up all the time. Children's books can be expensive, but there are corners you can cut. Many bookstores and publishers sell very attractive children's books in inexpensive paperback editions. In addition, much is available free on the Internet. I urge you to send for the catalogues of major children's paperback publishers and take advantage of their low mail-order rates. Other good sources of inexpensive children's books are supermarkets, discount stores, book clubs, and book fairs. Be alert for used book sales and garage sales.

A comment is in order here about the values· exemplified in much of children's literature. There is, truly, much to object to in many of the old standbys. In this area, as in any questions of value, one parent may sharply disagree with another about what is or is not appropriate for children. Familiar works of children's literature have been attacked as violent, racist, sexist, militaristic, and so on.

(I was appalled not long ago when I reread some of my own child-hood books.) I urge you to look beyond the colorful pictures at what a book really says about values. I do not mean, however, that you should always shield your student from stories whose values you disagree with—I think it's sometimes better to go ahead and read the story, but talk about the issue honestly.*

Having books on hand and easily available to your child will do much of the teaching. By reading ABC books with your pupil from time to time—and having them around for her to read by herself—you'll find that she learns many of the letters without much outright teaching.

5. Writing & scribbling

Your student should have ample writing material at hand, supplies he can get to without having to ask. I prefer to keep paper and writing utensils in several places in the classroom and in the house—in the bedroom, kitchen, den, etc. Provide him with a chalkboard and plenty of chalk, his own private supply of pencils (or washable felt-tip pens or crayons), and paper. I prefer regular No. 2 pencils—not too sharp. I also like the specially designed "Dr. Grip" mechanical pencils, manufactured by Pilot Pen Company and available in many office supply stores. These encourage the child to grip the pencil properly, without "choking up."

To begin with, you should buy unlined paper. Once your student has begun to write in earnest—around Kit 3—you might begin encouraging the use of wide-lined paper. (Beginner paper is available by mail and in many drug and discount stores.)

Whether your student uses a chalkboard or unlined paper, at this stage she will probably be doing a great deal more scribbling

---

* Here is a way *not* to do it. My son Frank, a full-fledged railroad buff at ages 3 and 4, thought the book *Tootle* was simply splendid. I, on the other hand, am convinced that its values are dreadful. After suffering in silence, on about the hundredth reading or so I just told him that I wasn't going to read *Tootle* any-more, to him or to anyone else. I should have told him honestly the first or second time *why* I didn't like the book.

than writing. Scribbling is a useful undertaking in and of itself; it is obviously good fun and may well be aesthetically pleasing to the child. Scribbling often seems to lead to writing, map making, sign making, and all sorts of great things. While some would regard scribbling as aimless, it is, in fact, an altogether worthwhile activity. You would do well to encourage it.

One good way to encourage a child's interest in writing is to write little notes specifically to him, on his chalkboard or elsewhere. Messages such as "Mommy loves Kevin," "Susan has a dirty face," or "Today we go to the zoo" have a high potential for drawing a response.

6. Writing together

Try writing stories together or getting your student to dictate stories for you to print or type (see Figure 6 on the next page). Then read the stories together. These can be simple accounts of your trips together to the store, the zoo, or someplace else, or they can be more fanciful. This sort of shared work gives you many opportunities to talk about written language—about letters, spelling, words, reading, etc. It can also be a great deal of fun, a thoroughly enjoyable joint endeavor. These stories are likely to become keepsakes for you; you won't believe the gems you'll come up with. It will benefit you both to become adept at story writing; besides being pleasurable, writing together is a highly successful learning strategy for many children.

You may use lined or unlined paper, as you choose. (My preference for unlined paper applies to kids, not adults.) Use all capital letters to begin with, while your student is getting to know capital letter names. When you finish Kit 1, you can begin to use both capital and lower-case printing for your stories.

Label and/or write captions on your student's paintings or other artwork. Ask "What is this painting?" or "What is this about?" and listen to the child's answer with respect. Forget art criticism. Possible captions include "Dragon eating an English muffin," "It is raining and the house is on fire," "This is a tree and a bird and an

Figure 6.

Figure 7.

alligator," and so on. You can also write the child's name on her artwork, or have her write it. Let her sign and date each one (WENDY 7/99, CHARLES, MARCH 3, 2005, etc.).

7. Things to make together

There are all sorts of things you and your student can make that involve words and letters and reading. Several ideas are described below.

a. *Letter scrapbook.* To make a letter scrapbook (see Figure 7), go through old newspapers and magazines with your student, and cut out several examples of each capital letter. Then sort them, and paste them into a scrapbook. (Take one or two pages per letter, and leave some space—you'll want to add lower-case letters and pictures later.) This is particularly useful in developing what psychologists call a "set for diversity"—an awareness that the printed forms representing a certain letter may vary widely.

b. *Letter displays and banners.* If you cut large (10" high) capital letters out of construction paper, the child can color them, paint them, or make a collage by pasting scraps of paper on them. Then you and she can mount them on stiff paper and hang them on the wall, or make a mural by mounting them on roll paper, butcher paper, or computer printout paper. Another option is to buy (or get a computer program that prints) banners with large letters.

c. *Salt or sand tray.* A salt tray—or sand tray, if you prefer—can be made by covering a shoebox top, cookie tray, or paper plate with a loose layer of salt or dry sand. Together with your student, practice writing letters in the salt or sand with one or two fingers. This method has great teaching advantages: it provides the child with both tactile and kinesthetic feedback. Moreover, it's cheap, it's easy, and you can erase it simply by shaking the tray a little from side to side.

d. *Finger painting.* Another activity I enjoy—one that causes
    many parents misgivings—is finger painting. Like fishing and
    watching sunrises, finger painting is clearly good for the soul.
    I admit that undertaking finger painting with an active four-
    year-old requires solid preparation and effective supervision,
    but the result is well worth the trouble. Of course, finger
    painting is plastic and imaginative, and you may not want to
    load it down with dull objectives, like "We're going to finger
    paint an *H* today." In the course of finger painting, the two
    of you can make all the *H*'s you want, but you should also
    make swirls and hand prints and flowers and snakes and all
    the other nifty things you can make in finger painting. Fin-
    ger paints and paper are commercially available at toy stores
    and school supply stores.

    A related activity is finger paint printing. Finger paint on
    a nonabsorbent plastic surface (a Formica counter top, for
    example, or a vinyl floor), and when you get something you
    want to keep (the letter H, maybe, or an especially good
    flower), carefully lay down a sheet of newsprint over the
    finger painting, press gently, and lift. (This is great for flow-
    ers and for letters like A, H, and W that do not face a special
    way. It does not work so well with *F, G, J, L, N, P, Q, R, S,*
    and *Z* because they come out backward.)

e. *Letter sculpting.* You and your student may also enjoy mak-
    ing capital letters out of Play-Doh or modeling clay. Roll the
    material out in "snakes," then twist it to form letters. This is
    extremely helpful in teaching letters that a child is having
    difficulty learning.

f. *Letter cookies.* You may enjoy making cookies either shaped
    like the letters or decorated with the letters in colored frost-
    ing, jimmies, or sprinkles. Stiff cookie dough will roll and
    twist into letter shapes rather like Play-Doh (I prefer a dry
    cookie mix for this project). These letters have a tendency to
    spread upon baking, but they are eaten with gusto. A fast,
    easy way to make letter cookies is to use a tube of frosting to

squirt letters on homemade or store-bought cookies. Letters can also be made by arranging raisins, M & Ms, or other candies on the damp surface of a cookie before it goes into the oven. I find that this works well.

8. Own words

I have already discussed the usefulness of teaching your student to recognize and perhaps write her own name in capital letters. She may also want to learn other words—a pet's name, your name, a familiar place name, etc. Print each of these words on an index card for your student, using all capital letters.

9. Sight words

Your student might learn to recognize certain common words by sight, whenever you encounter them in your reading. In later kits these words will include many important but oddly spelled words— such as *here, said, come, were, their,* and so on. For right now, try working on the capital letter words *I* and *A,* as well as initial abbreviations—*TV, EDT, PM, NFL, CBS,* etc. Watch for these in your reading together; when you come to such a word, point it out and read it together with your student, or let her read it.

The purpose of all this is to show your student that there are words he can read, and that there will be more and more of them— that reading is not an exclusively grown-up activity, but rather, is something that he can learn to do. He should come to feel that there are words that are *his,* and that he can learn more and more of them.*

---

* One of the early reading experiences I remember most fondly is sitting on my father's lap as he read *Man in a Chemical World,* the two of us trying to find *my* words in it. I still have the book; it is one of my treasures.

10. Games

There are several games you can play to help your pupil learn the letters. These games are ordinarily played just for fun. Be careful not to add any pressure to them.

a.   *Win-my-cards game.* Make a stack of letter cards and turn through them one at a time. As you place each card face up in a pile, the child has a chance to win your card by naming the letter. Those she names correctly she gets to keep. Those she misses you keep (once you tell her the name of the letter she missed). At the end of the game, count up her score (the number of cards she won). It helps to ham it up, with exaggerated anguish or glee—especially as she gets more and more cards from your dwindling supply. You're both working toward the day when she will win all the cards.

   Note: Always begin with a limited set of cards—the ones your student knows, and a few others that she might or might not know. The child should almost always get more cards than you do. Add cards as you go along.

b.   *"This is/show me/what is" game.* This game teaches new letters using a Montessori technique for exposing children to new things. First show the child a letter card, introduce the letter, and ask him to repeat the letter name ("This is *A*. Say *A*."). After the child says the letter name, talk with him about the distinctive features of the letter (calling attention to the sharp point, the two legs, the bridge, and anything else that seems remarkable and might be interesting to him). Be sure to mention the letter name often. Encourage your student to trace the letter with his finger, and then ask him to identify the letter again ("Show me *A*. Say *A*.").

   Once he has done this, praise him and express satisfaction. Then point to the letter one more time and ask, "What is this?" Hopefully he will name the correct letter, but it doesn't always work out that way. If he doesn't, don't worry or show disapproval. Just go back over the features again, and try to clear up any confusion. Then drop the subject and plan to return to it later. Don't run it into the ground.

c. *Letter-of-the-day game.* Each day, ask your student to pick a letter (choosing from the letter cards or poster) to be her special letter that day. After she picks one, make it your business to help her find the letter in signs, newspaper ads, posters, Web pages, labels, TV commercials, letterheads, book titles, magazines, etc. I suspect you will both find considerable pleasure and surprise exploring all the places you can find letters. (Be advised that *Q* and *Z* are tough—first pick some easy ones, like *E, A, O, S, R, T, M,* and *N.*)

Once your student has selected a letter for the day, she keeps the card for that letter in a special spot—in her cubby, on her dresser, the chalkboard, the refrigerator door, etc.

d. *Letters-on the-tree game.* As the child learns letters, tack or tape the cards for those letters on his wall or on a bulletin board in a tree-like array. If you like, draw a tree with branches on a large sheet of paper or posterboard. Then put the letters on the branches as they are learned.

e. *Grab bag game.* This game is a great favorite. To play, you will need a No. 6 brown paper bag, or a small cloth bag measuring about 6 x 10". (I prefer to avoid plastic bags with kids.) You'll also need 52 two-inch squares of white cardboard marked with two sets of uppercase letters (and numbered randomly from one to five on the reverse), as well as four red squares, four green squares, and a game board (laid out on a large sheet of paper, posterboard, or tagboard—a legal-size folder spread open is perfect). Finally, you will need small pieces to move around the board. Bolts, thimbles, rocks, or small plastic toys will do fine. (See Figure 8 on the next page.)

To begin the game, put all the squares into the bag, and draw to see who goes first. The player drawing the higher number starts (in case of a tie, draw again). On each turn, a player

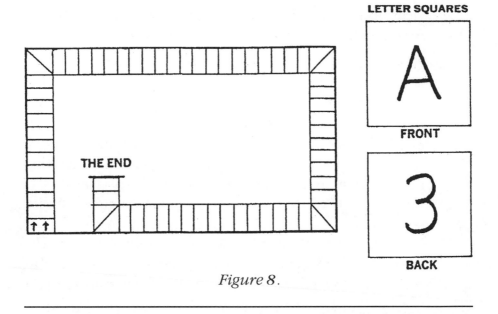

Figure 8.

draws a square from the bag, names the letter, and then moves his or her piece the number of places indicated on the back of the square. (In hard-nosed games, if you can't name the letter fairly quickly, you don't get to move. I prefer a more generous way of playing, waiting until the child can name the letter—with a little help, perhaps. Natural kid impatience will usually provide ample motivation and curiosity.)

A player loses a turn if he draws a red square, and gains an extra turn if he draws a green square. (In a variation of this game, you place alternating green and red dots every five spaces on the board. Players landing on a green dot get an extra turn, and players landing on a red dot lose a turn.)

As each square is drawn, it is put aside (not returned to the bag). If you use all the squares before someone reaches *The End*, replace them in the bag and keep playing. The game is over when a player reaches *The End*. (Make your own rules about whether you need to land directly on *The End* to win.)

There are letter learning games available in stores and on the Internet. Also, don't be afraid to experiment with your own letter games. Games you invent will probably be the best suited for you and your pupil.

11. Mail & e-mail

E-mail and the postal service can be valuable allies in teaching a child to read. In later kits we will consider all sorts of activities involving your student in writing and receiving mail. For now, a solid first step would be to subscribe to one of the several good magazines available for young children. These are usually not expensive, and they have interesting stories, games, and puzzles that you can read through together. In addition, there are a number of promising Web sites for children.

Also of great interest to some children is *National Geographic for Children.* This is brief and inexpensive, but lavishly illustrated with color photographs. The accompanying text is likely to be too advanced for your child, but the photography might be just the thing.

12. Media

You may find television useful in helping your student learn the letters. I am distrustful of TV, especially in large doses, and especially for children more than 6 years old. However, when carefully controlled and monitored, and viewed in moderation (no more than an hour per day), television can enrich your student's world.

A number of creative children's programs are produced on PBS and the educational channels. These lively programs pay varying amounts of attention to letter learning, and are usually fun to watch together. *Sesame Street* is especially good, and worth making a special effort to watch with the child. If need be, you can videotape segments for replay at more convenient times.

13. Pacing instruction

If your pupil continues to have trouble learning and remembering letter names, take this as a warning to *go slowly.* It often takes substantial periods of time for young children to learn the letters. Please don't rush.

With our present state of knowledge about learning disabilities, it is hard for even the most expert clinician to diagnose reading disabilities in preschool children. Since the incidence of a reading or learning disability is estimated at 1 in 10 boys, and perhaps 1 in 50 girls,* parents are well advised to keep in mind that their child *could* have such a disability.

I advise parents to seek a learning disabilities evaluation if their child (1) has difficulty acquiring beginning reading skills at home (learning letter names and letter-sound associations, or recognizing familiar words as wholes) *and* (2) continues to have difficulty with reading after she starts school. Such an evaluation is especially important if there is a family history of reading problems, or if the child has a history of speech or auditory difficulties. It can be provided by the public school system or by the private or religious school the child attends or will attend. Alternatively, facilities for such testing are usually available at colleges and universities; often community colleges will have facilities that are both professional and inexpensive. Another alternative path in testing is to seek the services of a qualified professional in private practice—usually a clinical or educational psychologist who specializes in diagnosis of learning problems. These specialists can be expensive, but their services can help significantly.

---

* Estimates in the literature vary widely. These figures are among the more conservative and seem about right to me. The existence of gender differences is of considerable interest, but is not fully understood. It seems likely that these differences are rooted in differences of neural organization and chemistry, as well as in culture and development.

🐝 *Kit 2: The lower-case letter names*

MATERIALS

- Lower-case letter poster
- Lower-case letter cards
- Plastic lower-case letters

GOAL

The purpose of this kit is to help your student learn the names of the lower-case letters. Go on to Kit 3 when your student can name all the lower-case letters in any order.

INSTRUCTIONS

1. What to do

This section provides a broad summary of Kit 2; each individual step will be treated in more detail in the following sections.

The first step is introducing your student to lower-case letters. Many authorities prefer that you call them *lower-case* instead of *little* or *small* because of the confusion that can result since some "little" letters—*f, b, l,* etc.—are as tall as the capitals. However, it can also be argued that the phrase *lower-case* has little meaning for a young child; it may be easier for children to understand the idea of *small, little,* or even *baby letters.* You are the best judge of whether it will confuse your student to call lower-case letters *small.* (Of course, it is always possible to explain later that *lower-case* is another name for the "little" letters.)

The best place to start learning the lower-case letters is with the letters the child already knows—those that closely resemble their capital letter forms. The letters *c, f, k, j, o, p, s, t, u, v, w, x, y,* and *z* will probably be learned rather quickly; perhaps the child already knows them by now. Find out which letters he knows by asking him, by playing the win-my-cards game, or through any other means you find useful.

Print the child's name for her twice, first using all capitals, and then using both capital and lower-case letters. Compare these two forms with her. Make a poster of the lower-case letters with their capital letter forms, and make lower-case letter cards. Teach your pupil to recognize her own name, as well as the word *a*.

Continue to read aloud with your student, and go to libraries and bookstores (and/or surf the Web) as often as you can manage. Write stories together, and encourage your student's scribbling and attempts to write. Leave printed notes and messages for him and work together on your homemade ABC book (now including lower-case letters).

Talk about the lower-case letters whenever a chance presents itself, and play letter learning games. Watch *Sesame Street* together, and talk about what you see. Also use the written language elsewhere in your environment—on signs, labels, headlines, books, magazines, etc.—to teach the letter names and to convey the idea that reading is both useful and pleasant.

When your student knows the names of all the lower-case letters, go ahead to Kit 3, even if you haven't completed (or even started) all the activities I suggest for Kit 2.

2. Things for you to make or buy

    a. Lower-case letter poster and wall strip. Following the general guidelines for poster making discussed in Kit 1, make a wall poster of the lower-case letters. Hang it near the capital letter poster from Kit 1.

        Figure 9 gives a chart of directions for printing the lower-case letters. This manuscript alphabet was deliberately selected to be easy for young children to recognize and print, and for its close similarity to the writing systems most commonly used in American schools and kindergartens.

        There are minor differences from publisher to publisher in handwriting systems for lower-case letters; some authori-

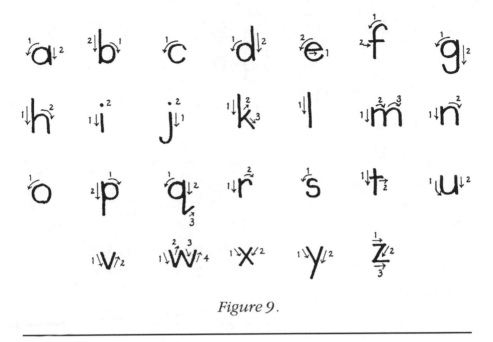

Figure 9.

ties give the *q* a tail, for instance, while others prefer it tail-less. However, none of these differences is likely to cause significant problems for your student; any difficulty he encounters should be easily reconciled.

Figure 10 (on the next page) shows two possible models for lower-case letter posters and one model for a wall strip. A combination poster is shown in Figure 11.

b. *Plastic lower-case letters.* As I advised in Kit 1, magnetized plastic letters have many uses and are well worth their small cost. You can buy these at most toy or discount stores.

c. *Lower-case letter cards.* You can make lower-case letter cards for Kit 2 using 3 x 5" index cards, a black marker, and a blue ball-point pen. Use the unlined sides of the cards and try to keep the size of the letters consistent. Use the same simplified alphabet you used on the poster. Be sure to draw a blue line for each letter to rest on. (See Figure 12, p. 39.)

d. *"Feelie" letters.* These are letters that your student can learn

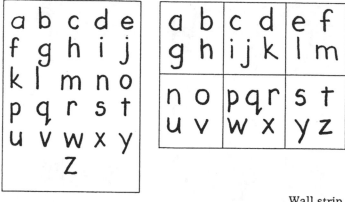

Wall strip

abcdefghijklmnopqrstuvwxyz

Figure 10.

Figure 11.

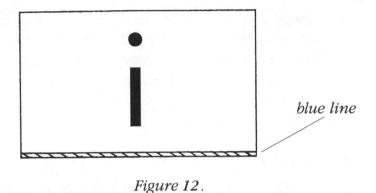

blue line

Figure 12.

---

to identify by touch as well as by sight. Brought to perfection by Maria Montessori, these are highly effective teaching materials. They are especially useful in teaching children the letters hardest for them to learn.

Feelie letters can be made in a number of ways and from a variety of materials. One of the easiest ways to make them is to draw each letter on paper toweling, cloth, construction paper, or another highly textured material, and then cut it out and paste it onto a smooth paper or cardboard surface. This creates a sharp contrast of "feel" between the letter and its background.

Have your student trace over each letter's shape with her fingers, really trying to get the feel of it. It sometimes helps to "follow the arrows"—to feel the letter as she might write it. You can also play blindfold games and other guessing games with these letters.

e. *Magic slate.* This old favorite—a slate with a dark waxed backing, covered by a grayish plastic sheet—is once again commercially available in toy stores. The child writes on the plastic sheet with a stylus, and when the sheet is lifted, the slate erases as if by magic. Presto! These toys have delighted many youngsters over the century or so they have been around. Get one if you can.

    f. *Computer.* You and your student can use various programs
to form letters with computers, often in color. By all means,
try this together, and if you have a color printer, print out the
results. Together, you can design a poster to suit your own
taste. Consider purchasing additional type fonts, which are
available at software stores.

3. Reading aloud

A basic requirement of this program is that you read aloud to your
student for at least 20 minutes every day, in circumstances as pleasant as you can manage. Reading for more than 20 minutes is fine—
up to the point when it starts to become a drag for one or both of
you, or threatens to swallow up all the child's playtime or all your
time together. (In my experience, what reading aloud mostly swal-
lows up is naptime.)

    Read from materials the child wants to hear. (Stock market quo-
tations, the philosophy of Kant, and current news from the Middle
East will not ordinarily qualify.) Several books provide advice on
selecting children's reading material (see the following section for
details), but the ultimate judges are you and your student. Don't
feel that you should enjoy a book just because it got an award or an
authority recommended it.

4. Books & magazines

Continue taking trips to the library with your student. Taking a child
on a special errand to get books for both of you conveys a clear
message about the importance of books, libraries, and reading.

    Give some thought to subscribing to a children's magazine. While
this is an added expense, it is also a nice experience for your student to have her very own magazine come in the mail. A subscrip-
tion makes a fine gift, one that keeps on coming, and can be suggested to grandparents or other relatives for birthdays and other
occasions.

    To learn more about children's literature, consult *Literature for
Children*, by M. Arbuthnot. You may also wish to look over current

and back issues of *The Horn Book,* a magazine for children's librarians, and the *Children's Library Bulletin.* In addition, the *New York Times Book Review* devotes two issues per year to children's books. Finally, *A Parent's Guide to Children's Reading* (1975), by Nancy Larrick, is a classic in the field; it is hard to find but well worth reading. Newer texts include *Children's Books Too Good To Miss,* by Harlow (1992), and *Best Books for Beginning Readers,* by Gunning (1997). Another good source is O'Dean's *Great Books for Girls* (1997).

5. Writing & scribbling

Check this section in Kit 1—make sure you have ample writing materials available to your pupil. You will probably want to set some limits about these materials and their use, as well as a few "don'ts." (My son Frank managed to make his mark indelibly on the door of our shared summer cottage, using a permanent black marker. His relatives were not happy about this.)

Don't be concerned with the form of any letters the child happens to make at this stage. You should be grateful for anything you can get. Most young children have real difficulty writing letters, and lower-case letters seem—and probably *are*—harder for them (though the Montessorians routinely teach 4- and 5-year-olds to write lower-case letters). If your student wants to learn, teach her to write these letters, but don't push it. Writing should be an entirely voluntary activity at this stage.

6. Writing together

As I discussed in Kit 1, there are many things you and your student can write together—by hand, on a computer, or on a typewriter. Your writing can be factual (e.g., a journal, an anecdote, an account of a party, trip, ball game, or other notable event). Or you can write fiction, perhaps putting into writing a favorite bedtime story. (I need not remind you that some of the very best children's literature was written that way.) My own stories have included the adventures of an imaginary friend or friends (a dragon who dotes on marshmallows, his friend the bird, and a boy whose name was first Frank and later became William), and a fantasy story of a prince named Sam who refuses to slay—and thus befriends—a dragon. (Dragons were very big around my place for a number of years.)

Let me try to persuade you to keep a journal together, in which you record the events of each day and any thoughts on your experiences. All you have to do is write a few lines each day. This will surely be a keepsake; it should make for fascinating reading at the time, and also when you go back and see what you did last month, last year, etc. Another advantage of this sort of writing is that it helps your child to learn the relationships of written and spoken language. When you dictate something, it can be written down and read back later in the same way it was spoken. In this way, writing "preserves" spoken language.

Be sure to include snapshots, drawings, ticket stubs, programs, and the like in your journal; this will add enormously to its appeal for you when you go back and read it later. Your journal will become a classic for both you and the child.

7. *Things to make together*

Every item you can make using capital letters (as described in Kit 1, Section 7) can also be made with lower-case letters.

Add lower-case letters cut from old magazines and newspapers to your letter scrapbook. Be sure to leave room for pictures, which will be added in Kit 3. You can also cut lower-case letters out of construction paper, then paint, color, or paste things on them, and mount them on contrasting paper. Hung up on a wall, on a bulletin board, or as part of a mural, these letters make a fine display.

If you feel really ambitious, you can make a letters bedspread, a letters quilt, or letter curtains; cut letter shapes out of scraps of cloth and sew them on a contrasting fabric backing. These crafts can be very attractive, and creating them together with a child can be a delightful learning activity. One Cambridge mother made such a bedspread with her son when he was sick, cutting the letters out with pinking shears and letting him place them on the spread before she sewed them on the machine. As with the journal, you not only have a fine learning experience; you are also creating a keepsake. That spread is now a family treasure. I also know preschool teachers who make a quilt each year with their class.

By all means, repeat with the lower-case letters any projects you enjoyed with capital letters. For example, if capital letter cookies worked well for you, make lower-case letter cookies too.

8. Own words

Write your student's name for him in both capitals and lower-case letters. (This is a good way to start teaching the lower-case letters; see Section 1.) Also use upper- and lower-case letters to write the names of family members, pets, and so on. The easiest way I know to explain capitals is to say, "Capital letters are used in a lot of ways, and one of the most important ways is to begin people's names." You need not go into a discussion of the rules for capitalization (unless, of course, your student insists).

You might go so far as to print the names of family members on place cards or napkins for the dinner table, or on other items to be distributed. Or you could ask your pupil to sort incoming mail into shoeboxes or plastic bins marked with each family member's name. I also like the idea of creating word cards, 3 x 5" or 5 x 8" index cards (or 3 x 11" construction-paper cards) with the child's own words printed on them.*

9. Sight words

In order to read simple children's books, your student will need to know a number of common words by sight. By learning to recog-

---

* If you have not read Sylvia Ashton-Warner's book *Teacher*, you probably should—not so much to learn pedagogical techniques, but because you deserve a treat. *Teacher* is a fine book, and in it you get to know Sylvia Ashton-Warner, as talented and sensitive a person as you're ever likely to encounter. One of the many ways she teaches is with "own words," on cards and elsewhere.

nize a few of these at a time, she will eventually come to know most of them.

In Kit 1 your student learned to recognize the single capital letter words *I* and *A*, as well as capitals used as abbreviations. In this kit we will concentrate on teaching your student to recognize the words *a* and *the* (or *The*). Watch for these words in your reading together or on signs, labels, TV, newspapers, and so forth.

Don't push your child to learn a lot of sight words just now—concentrate on getting the letters straight and learning to recognize the words *I, A, a, the,* and *The.*

10. Games

You can use lower-case letters to play any of the games discussed in Kit 1. The *win-my-cards game* is a good one to use, adding a few lower-case letters at a time. *"This is/show me/what is"* is a particularly effective method for teaching difficult letters. The *grab bag game* is also easily adapted to lower-case letters. Add lower-case squares (with high number values) to the capitals, until you have all 26 lower-case letters. You might want to take out some of the best-known capital letters as the number of lower-case squares grows; this way, the game will move more quickly and the lower-case letters will get more attention.

The *letter-of-the-day game* is an all-around winner—especially after your student has learned the capitals and is working on the lower-case letters. This game leads easily into the *letters-on-the-tree* routine: the letter selected at the beginning of the day gets talked about and looked for all day, and by bedtime or the end of the school day, it should be known well enough to put on the tree.

Once your student begins learning lower-case letters, you can also introduce the *matching game*. There are commercially available computer programs that run matching games, but you can easily set the game up yourself. The child can play this alone or with you assisting (although when he first starts playing, it's probably best for you to be there to help). To begin, spread out the capital letter cards, face up, on one side of the child, and place the lower-case letters face up on the other side. The child's task is to match each upper-case letter to its lower-case form. Playing together, take turns pairing up letters until all have been matched. When more than one child is playing, you may wish to keep score by counting the number of pairs matched by each player. This is rarely necessary, however, and can create a negative experience for whoever "loses." I prefer not to keep score this way.

11. Mail & e-mail

As I pointed out in Kit 1, mail can be a formidable ally in teaching a child about written language. Let your student sort incoming mail for various family members and route incoming e-mail to the proper recipient. I suggested in Kit 1 that you subscribe to some magazines for the child, so that some mail will come directly to her. Now and then, you might also send her a note yourself. Try enlisting relatives and friends in this effort; you may find a pen pal with unsuspected talent. Since cards and letters have to be answered, they provide a natural reason for your pupil to combine written and spoken language in composing replies for you to write down. And e-mail has a wonderful ease and immediacy that makes it ideal for a child's correspondence.

With little effort, you can develop a burgeoning correspondence for your student. This should increase her interest in writing and reading, and show her that these can be useful tools for *her*.

12. Media

In Kit 1, I suggested that you and your student watch *Sesame Street* often. Continue watching this program, and consider buying a record of the alphabet song (or any other letter songs you can find). Try to teach your student the alphabet song, if he doesn't already know it. You can sing it together, pointing to the letters on the poster. This is a splendid bedtime or naptime activity, and I heartily recommend it. The song is best learned after your student has learned the upper-case letter names, so that you avoid the misconception in so many kids' minds that *LMNOP* is one letter.

Still another option—and this is a mind-blower—is to make a videotape or animated movie of the letters, using plastic cut-out letters, a tripod, lights, a video camera that has a "single frame" setting, and much patience. To make an animated movie, take one still shot at a time and move the letters slightly with each shot. Figure out how you want the letters to move, and what background you would like. A splendid book about making animated films is *Teaching Film Animation to Children*, by Yvonne Anderson (1971), but this appears to be out of print and available only in libraries. A good current source is Grisante's *Video Making for Kids* (1996).

🌱 *Kit 3: Introducing letter-sound associations*

MATERIALS

- Black and red felt-tip pens
- Pencil
- 3 x 5" index cards
- ABC books

GOALS

The goal of this kit is to get your student to associate sounds with most of the letters.* It is not important that your student learn all of the letter sounds just yet, but by the time you move to Kit 4 he should be reasonably clear on three points:

1. Letters can stand for sounds.
2. Words have sounds in them.
3. Words have "beginning sounds."

INSTRUCTIONS

1. What to do

One of the best tools for making children aware of letter-sound associations is the traditional ABC book. There are many of these available commercially, as well as in libraries, and later in this kit I will describe how you can make your own from cut-up magazines and newspapers.

---

* If your child substitutes one sound for another when speaking, or can't say certain speech sounds, prudence and common sense dictate that you not push him to speak these sounds "properly." For example, a child who says *th* for *s* should not be expected to say "*s* is for *snake*" as you would say it. The reply "*eth* ith for *thnake*" is entirely acceptable. A child can read and understand a

When your pupil is in the mood and you have time, sit down for a few minutes and read an ABC book together. Let him tell you what each letter is "for" (e.g., "*k* is for *kangaroo*"), or what letter certain words begin with. Posters and wall strips for teaching letter-sound associations can be bought inexpensively or constructed fairly easily on your own. Also easy to make are movable alphabet cards, which you should begin using in this kit and continue to use throughout the program.

While working with this kit and the next, try to increase the amount of time you and your pupil read aloud each day. When possible, read aloud for 15 to 20 minutes twice a day. Try to hold the book so that the child can see it. And if you are reading aloud to more than one child, be sure to include each pupil by asking questions of her and making frequent eye contact. You can begin talking about letter sounds very naturally, making a transition from your games of "What's that letter?" and "Can you find an *s* on this line?" to "What's the letter that says '*sss*' in *Sesame Street?*" Also keep a journal with your student, and continue to encourage her to dictate stories to you. As mentioned in earlier kits, journals can be excellent teaching devices and delightful references to use later on.

You can also play "beginning sounds" games with your student. I like the "I'm thinking of something that begins with __" game, and youngsters still think the "I'm going to Boston" game is delightful. In Section 10, I describe these and several other games that have been played successfully by parents and small children for many years.

One note of caution should be kept in mind with regard to all the activities in this kit: sounds to be associated with the letters vary significantly in some cases. You might point out that the letters *c, g, a, e, i, o, u,* and *y* sometimes represent other sounds, but that for

---

sound without being able to say it. Most, though not all, speech difficulties are developmental and are resolved without therapy. Many speech problems *do* require professional diagnosis and treatment, though. If your child has a speech irregularity, have him checked by age 5 by a qualified speech professional. If therapy is indicated, you should get on with it early, rather than putting it off.

now you'll concentrate on learning just one sound for each letter. When ambiguity exists explain it,* but at this point in the program, the speech sounds associated with the letters should be as follows:

> *a* as in *alligator*
> *c* as in *cat*
> *e* as in *egg*
> *g* as in *go*
> *i* as in *if*
> *o* as in *octopus*
> *u* as in *uncle*
> *y* as in *yes*

Another difficulty to be aware of is that when you teach certain sounds (e.g., "*c* says *kuh*"), you're including a sound that the letter doesn't actually say. This can lead to some problems later on. For instance, a child putting sounds together can encounter difficulty getting *cat* out of "*kuh-aa-tuh*." This sort of blending can be taught, but you need to know beforehand that the problem exists. One way to minimize it is to cut letter sounds off as sharply as you can. Practice trying to minimize extra sounds when you pronounce *p, t, g, b, k, h, j,* and other potentially problematic consonants.

When your student has made a fair amount of progress in learning the sounds, and has at least tried playing the games described above, move gradually into Kit 4. Try to make certain that your student understands the three concepts outlined on the first page of this kit.

2. Things for you to make or buy

> *a. Movable alphabet cards.* A movable alphabet—consisting of letters printed on small squares that are moved about to form words—was devised by Maria Montessori for her Casa dei Bambini in Italy. There is also some evidence that mov-

---

* Occasionally, in ABC books or elsewhere, you're going to encounter different sounds—*g* for *giraffe*, perhaps, or *e* for *eagle*. The explanation given above is an honest statement of the facts, and is usually sufficient.

able letters were used by Athenian tutors in classical times. Today, these materials are used widely in Montessori schools, in commercial reading programs, and in computer learning programs and games. Eventually you and your student will be able to form numerous words in succession simply by changing letters around. For instance, suppose the child starts with the letters *m-a-n,* spelling *man.* He can then replace the *m* with *p* (*pan*), interchange *p* with *n* (*nap*), replace *n* with *m* (*map*), and so on.

Considerably more flexible than workbooks or other text materials, the movable alphabet is very well suited to teaching young children. It lends itself well to games and informal learning situations. And it can be used by one child working alone, by a child and a tutor, or by small groups of children and adults. This program utilizes a special homemade version of the movable alphabet, printed on 3 x 5" index cards with red and black felt-tip pens. In Kits 3 and 4 we begin by associating speech sounds with the letters.

The first step in creating the cards is drawing the "baseline," a light pencil line 3 inches from the top of each card. This line helps you to center the letters and to align the cards when you put them together. A quick way to draw the baseline is to use another 3 x 5" card as a ruler. If you place the second card horizontally over the first card, you can draw a line exactly 3 inches from the top of the first card (see Figure 13).

Next print letters on the cards. Use the red marker for the vowels *a, e, i, o,* and *u,* and the black marker for the other letters. In printing the letters, remember to use the simplified letter forms. With a little practice, you can make reasonable approximations of these forms. Some of these (*m, n, c,* etc.) should be about 1½ inches high, and others (*p, t, g,* etc.) should be about 2½ inches high.

Finished cards should look as shown in Figure 14. You may make cards with capital letters, but they are not necessary.

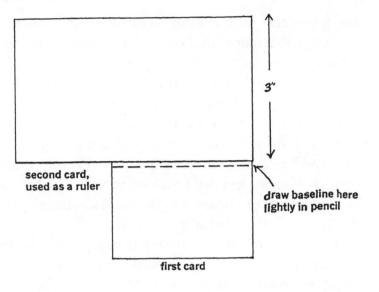

second card, used as a ruler

3″

draw baseline here lightly in pencil

first card

Figure 13.

Figure 14.

b. *Letter-sound association poster or wall strip.* You can buy a letter-sound association poster or wall strip, or you can make one yourself—either drawing the pictures (they don't have to be all that good) or cutting them out of magazines. (My strong preference, if cut-out pictures are used, is to make the poster together with the child, letting her cut and paste wherever possible.)

I like the idea of using a simple set of word associations, associating a single familiar noun with each letter. The list given below is designed with young children in mind and features nouns selected for familiarity. If a word seems inappropriate for your student, feel free to substitute one of your own. (You might feel like substituting *yolk*, say, for *yoyo*, or *lion* for *ladder*, or *Oscar*—of *Sesame Street* fame—for *octopus*. This is fine; go ahead.)

The layout of an ABC poster is important. The objects need to be very clearly associated with the letters; the last thing you need here is confusion. My preference is to divide the poster into 26 letter blocks, with each block including one picture and both the capital and lower-case forms of the letter.

You can make a poster or a letter strip, or both. Using either of these makes learning the letter-sound associations much easier. If you just can't complete either of these yourself, consider purchasing one.

A apple	J jet	S snake
B boy	K key	T table
C cat	L ladder	U umbrella
D dog	M man	V vase
E elephant	N nail	W woman
F fish	O octopus	X x-ray (exit?)
G girl	P penny	Y yo-yo
H hat	Q quarter	Z zipper
I Indian	R ring	

3. Reading aloud

I mentioned earlier that when working with this kit and the next one, you should try to have your student read more than 20 minutes daily, if you can possibly manage it. Reading for an average of 30 minutes or more per day is very helpful, especially if it is done in more than one sitting. Enlist other adults in the child's world to read aloud to her.

Don't let my urging you to spend more time reading make you read when your student really doesn't want you to. Be careful to keep the experience pleasant, desirable. Whatever you do, don't let reading aloud get to be a chore—at least not for your student. (There may be occasions—a good many of them, perhaps—when there are things you'd rather do than sit down and read *Peter Rabbit* for the 35th time to a child whose motivation, you suspect, has something to do with putting off bedtime.) Reading aloud should be emotionally warm, too, and supportive. I think you should hold your kids when you read to them, or at least sit next to them.*

4. Books & magazines

You would do well to get several ABC books from libraries, bookstores, or the collections of friends whose children have outgrown them. But please do not restrict your reading aloud to ABC books; this can get dull for both of you. Leave ABC books with your student at naptime, or at odd moments during the day, or prominently displayed in the book corner.

Sesame Street and Disney books and magazines, as well as supermarket workbooks, feature the letters prominently, and are lively and colorful. In the past, a number of *Sesame Street* posters and other promotional items have been given away, but these may not be available any longer. Try to locate free materials by contacting

---

* With no evidence at all, I am still convinced that one of the main reasons I enjoy reading so much is that I long ago associated the love, warmth, and closeness of my parents and grandmother reading aloud to me with reading itself. Now when I read, I feel good, loved, safe, and okay, and the world backs off a little bit. This is escapist beyond question, but it works for me.

the TV station in your area that carries the *Sesame Street* broadcasts, looking for giveaway offers in magazines, and searching the Internet for material to download.

Occasionally, try reading aloud brief parts of newspaper articles or other materials that you think might interest your student. Don't overdo it. Mainly, you should still be reading what your student wants to hear or what you feel fairly certain he will like. Current politics and international affairs are usually not included.

5. *Writing & scribbling*

Keep writing your student notes, especially on his chalkboard. If you are the child's teacher, try putting notes in his cubby, in the pocket of his coat, or on the back of his drawings. If you are the child's parent, you could also tuck notes away under his pillow, in among his pajamas, beside his breakfast plate, or on a bulletin board or other family message center. If you don't have a family message center, try establishing one. All it takes is a chalkboard or bulletin board in a central place where each member of the family looks for messages and announcements. (We have used the refrigerator door for years.) Having a place on the board and actually getting messages is a big deal for a 4-year-old—especially if there are other children who get messages too.

Lacking a message center, you might do well to establish another regular place where your student can expect to find notes from you. Most classrooms have a bulletin board for this purpose.

Encourage your student to write and scribble at any opportunity. Set aside quiet times to write or draw at a table together. Also keep crayons, pencils, and paper around the kitchen, so that a child underfoot can be set to drawing at the kitchen table. You should be getting somewhere by now in teaching your student to write her name. Concentrate on that for now. Even if it's scrawled, progress is progress. Encourage scribbling, drawing, and everything in between. Keep steady in the faith that someday, something legible will emerge.

6. Things to make together

a. *Letter scrapbook.* Work on the letter scrapbook, cutting out pictures from magazines and pasting them in the appropriate pages. You may also find computer clip-art to be useful. Try to get pictures of several items for each letter (e.g., apples, alligators, airplanes, etc.).

This scrapbook can be an ongoing activity—you need not feel any sense of urgency about "getting it finished." Finding a picture for the scrapbook might fit nicely into your letter-of-the-day game. (It is possible to have the child sort through a folder of pictures you have already torn out, rather than having her go through old magazines every day.)

b. *Photo album.* Keep a photo album with your student, and consult together on what to write beside each picture. Be sure to print captions for maximum legibility.

c. *Journal.* You and your pupil should be maintaining a journal together. Seize any occasion to write something directly related to your student. If possible, do the writing in her presence and take her advice into account. Read what you write aloud as you are writing it, and then read it again after you've finished. Or have her dictate it to you.

d. *Writing scrapbook.* It is a good idea to keep the stories you write together in a scrapbook that your student can get to easily. Stories may be illustrated with artwork done by you and your student, in margins or on adjoining pages. This can become one of your student's favorite books; most children delight in reading about themselves. A portfolio or even a large envelope or folder can serve as a scrapbook. However you organize the stories, you should keep them readily accessible for rereading by your student at times you are not able to supervise closely.

e. *Diskette files.* Consider entering your journal onto a computer, either by keyboard or by scanner. You can save the entries on a special disk that the child can get to, rerun over and over, and print out at will. Indeed, it can even be printed out, bound, and saved (and copied for the child's grandparents).

8. Own words

Encourage your student to ask to learn words of her own. As previously discussed, these words should be important to her. If she can't think of any, you might suggest a few possibilities, but be careful not to oversell a word, or oversell the whole idea. These should be the child's words.

Print each word with a felt-tip pen on an index card or a piece of tagboard. Alternatively, let her keep her words in a notebook of her own, in which you also write a story now and then.

9. Sight words

For Kit 3, the sight word to be learned is *and*. (The capitalized form, *And*, occurs only rarely, and can be learned later.) Make a note of the word *and* in your reading, talk about it, spell it, and encourage your student to try to find other places where the word is used. Point out the word *and* on labels, on signs, and in newspapers—whenever it seems appropriate to you. Keep at it as you read together, but *keep this exercise a game.* Please don't make a big fuss over whether or not the child can recognize the word *and*, and please, *pretty* please, don't let your eagerness to teach interfere with the pleasure of reading together. Remember to make this your student's word, not just an assignment you're imposing on him. Enjoy.

10. Games

a. *I'm thinking of something that begins with _.* This game is usually played with some restrictions on the things the adult can be thinking of. You might limit your focus to things in the room, on a shelf, in a drawer, seen from a window, or in a picture. All that's necessary is that your student know what the limits are. Consider this example:

"I'm thinking of something on the kitchen table that begins with *s*."

"Salt."

"Good for you! Okay, smarty, I'm thinking of something else on the kitchen table that begins with *s*."

"Spoon."

"Great! I'm still thinking of something on the kitchen table that begins with *s*."

"Sugar."

One tip: Don't overdo it. Be sure you demonstrate your surprise and pleasure when your pupil figures out what you were thinking of, but don't show impatience with "wrong" or "foolish" answers. Try to see why the child answers as she does.

b. *I'm-going-to-Boston game.* In this game, the players take turns going through the alphabet, naming an object beginning with each letter in turn. For example, you might begin by saying, "I'm going to Boston, and I'm taking an *apple*." The child might then say, "I'm going to Boston, and I'm taking a *baby*," and you could respond, "I'm going to Boston, and I'm taking a *cat*."

And so the game goes. It requires some sophistication, as well as some hints from you about which letters come next. Once kids understand this game, however, they seem to like it. And so do I.

c. *How many things can we find that begin with __?* For this game, you and the child try to think of words that begin with a particular sound. You have to be a bit watchful here, because of the pitfalls in our language and spelling. If you're doing *s* and the child says, "*ceiling*," you ought to say, "Okay, fine. What else?" Don't make an issue of it. In time, your pupil will learn how to spell *ceiling* correctly. A related problem is that children may hear letters in a word that aren't in the spelling. For instance, some children might insist that *juice* be-

gins with a *d*. If you listen to yourself say the word, you'll notice
a hint of a *d* there, and many a child pronounces the word
"*duce*." So be wary of thinking that a child's answer is stupid or
wrong just because it isn't the one you expect. Amen.

d. *Letter-sound-of-the-day game.* This game is a variation of
    the letter-of-the-day game described in Kits 1 and 2. Each
    day you ask the child to pick a letter to focus on that day.
    Whenever he notices a word that begins with that letter—
    either in speech or in print—express hearty approval.

e. *Win-my-cards game.* As in Kits 1 and 2, in this game you
    turn through a few of the movable alphabet cards, one by
    one. In this kit, the child wins each card for which she can
    give an appropriate sound or word association (for *s*, for
    example, either *snake* or *sss* would be okay). At the end of
    the game, count her cards with her. You can both exult about
    her winning so many, looking forward to the great day when
    she finally wins them all.

f. *Grab bag game.* There are several ways to modify this game
    to help teach letter-sound associations. The easiest way is
    simply to change the rules: in addition to naming the letter
    drawn from the bag, players should give a word that begins
    with that letter. Another option is to add squares with simple
    drawings of the words listed in Section 2b of this kit, and
    remove the squares with the letters that begin these words.
    (Place the numbers from the backs of the removed squares
    on the backs of the corresponding picture squares.) The
    player's task is to name both the picture and its beginning
    letter. For example, if the child draws a square from the bag
    with a picture of a key on it, she should name both the pic-
    ture (*key*) and the letter associated with it (*k*).

11. Mail & e-mail

Keep an eye out for special offers that you and your student can
read about and send away for. My own experience with offers from

magazines, the Internet, television, comic strips, and cereal boxes has been mixed—a few outright winners are offset by an equal number of losers. Nevertheless, I think it is useful for your student to read these offers with you and learn to fill out an occasional order blank. I'm not sure that the long period of waiting for the merchandise to arrive serves any useful purpose, but receiving items ordered through the mail does demonstrate how useful writing can be. (E-mail, with its wonderful immediacy, cuts sharply into this waiting time. Use it, by all means.)

I have always found freebies more satisfactory to order than products that cost money—both for my philosophy and for my wallet. Several books (such as *Official Freebies for Kids;* 6th edition, 1998) are available through your bookstore which list all sorts of free things—posters, pictures, films, samples, pamphlets, etc.—that you and your student might enjoy. By all means, buy one of these books and send off for things together.

Getting your student interested in mail and other forms of correspondence should be a high priority; this kind of activity very clearly conveys the message that writing and reading are useful and worthwhile, and that they can lead to good things.

12. Media

In previous kits I have suggested that you and your child watch *Sesame Street* or other worthwhile programs you enjoy. (I also have expressed misgivings about children watching too much TV—I recommend limiting television viewing to an average of 30 minutes per day, except for special occasions.*) Whatever shows you choose, it is important that you actually watch them with your student and discuss them with her. Invite her opinions, and listen carefully to what she says. Consider the values involved, as well as the concepts being taught.

---

* Fanatics like me who have been known by their families to watch televised football for many hours a day around New Year's may expect some credibility problems when discussing limitations on television exposure.

✿ *Kit 4: Learning letter-sound associations*

MATERIALS

- Movable alphabet cards
- Books, magazines, and newspapers
- Computer
- ABC books
- Poster or wall strip

GOAL

The goal of this kit is to help your student associate speech sounds with each of the letters. He will not need to know *all* the sounds each letter represents. Move to Review Lesson I when he is regularly able to give one sound for each letter.

In order to learn to read, your student should have some understanding of seven basic ideas. The first three were discussed in Kit 3. The remaining four concepts are as follows:

4. Words are written with letters—you put letters together to make written words.
5. Words are spoken by saying sounds—you put sounds together to speak words.
6. Words can be spoken or written. You can write any word you can speak, and you can say any word you can write.
7. Words have "beginning" sounds, and often have "middle" and "ending" sounds as well.

INSTRUCTIONS

1. What to do

Keep reading aloud to your pupil, and venture into poetry and nursery rhymes if you haven't already done so. (Since Kit 5 will use rhymes and rhyming games, reading poetry occasionally at this stage may prove helpful as well as pleasant.)

Work on learning the letter sounds and associating key words with each letter. Directions are given in this kit for making a clothesline mobile, and for several games you can play. Use some of your odd moments to teach the sight word *you,* following my suggestions from previous kits or devising a strategy of your own. Remember to keep the learning fun, and engage in these activities only when your student wants to.

You should add to—and perhaps finish—your ABC scrapbook, and keep it where the child can look at it and show it to his friends. Refer to it from time to time, demonstrating its importance to you. Continue writing with your pupil—collaboratively or through dictation—and encourage his attempts at writing. Print out computer-written journals or stories for her to "read."

In all the activities of this kit, try to make sure your student understands the seven basic ideas mentioned earlier.* How can you tell whether she understands these concepts? One way, of course, is to ask her. Another is to discuss the way people talk, using their larynx, lips, tongue, teeth, and so on, to make the various sounds. Yet another way to teach the concepts is to mention them from time to time, watching your pupil to see if she understands. Many a child can understand these concepts operationally before she can remember how to articulate them. Your task is to explain each concept and discuss it with your pupil until you are content that she understands it well enough to use it.

If your student doesn't seem to understand or care about the last four concepts, be sure you're not pushing her. Wait a while,

---

* However, these concepts need not be mastered before you move on to Kit 5.

and keep working on the letters and sounds. She will need to understand these concepts in order to read in the fullest sense of the word, but she will gain this understanding sooner or later. Don't push or show impatience, whatever you do. Many young children find it quite difficult to think of words as divisible, and these children may also have trouble putting sounds together to form words. If your pupil encounters difficulty at this point, ease up on teaching these concepts. Some children learn the concepts only after they have begun reading words. Easy does it.

When your student can give a speech sound or word for each letter, move on to Review Lesson I. In fact, it is perfectly all right to move into the review lesson even if there are still several letter sounds that give your student trouble. It is better to keep moving than to bore the child.

2. Things for you to make or buy

a. *Homemade alphabet scrapbook.* Continue cutting out or drawing pictures to go with each letter. You should have several words to associate with most letters by now. Please remember the notes on which letter sounds to use for letters that have several pronunciations. Below are some common words that you may wish to associate with each letter.

A	apple, alligator, astronaut, actor, actress, andiron, ant (aunt)
B	boy, baby, bed, ball, bag, baloney, bubble gum, balloon, bank
C	cat, cap, cape, can, candy, car, cook, cookie, cop, cup
D	dog, dandelion, dirty, dirt, dust, daisy, dig
E	elephant, egg, echo, exit, end, elevator, escalator
F	flag, fox, friend, foot, fender, frame, fix, fig, flag, food
G	girl, goat, garbage, go, goofy, gorilla, get, golf
H	hat, horn, hop, hope, hanger, hockey, hustle, hiccup, hoof, hand
I	Indian, igloo, itch, icky, ink, in, into, inch

J	jet, jump, jump-rope, junk, jiggle, jungle, jog, jingle, jar
K	key, kangaroo, kite, king, kick, kiss
L	ladder, lamp, lion, lasso, loop, letter, lips, leg
M	man, money, monkey, mixer, matches, muffin, mop, mat
N	nail, nickel, needle, no, never, nasty
O	octopus, ox, Oscar, olive
P	penny, patch, pitch, pin, pan, pot, potato, pansy, petunia, pinch, pet, pig
Q	quarter, queen, quick, quit, quilt
R	ring, rocket, rip, roof, run, rag, red, rub
S	sock, smoke, sandwich, sand, sing, song, stop, snake, slip, sled, sugar
T	table, top, tiger, toes, tiptoe, train
U	umbrella, ugly, up
V	vase, violin, violet, very, victory
W	woman, wax, win, witch, wick, wet, wash, watch, world
X	x-ray (*box, exit, ax, ox, fox, Max, fix, etc.*)*
Y	yoyo, yellow, yolk, you, yes, yummy
Z	zipper, zombie, zoom, zoo, zigzag, zebra

b. *Clothesline mobile.* To create a clothesline mobile, collect objects or small pictures representing each of the letters and an associated word (see Figure 15 on the next page). For instance, to represent the first five letters of the alphabet, you could hang up a small plastic (or real) apple, and pictures or small figurines of a boy, a cat, a dog, and an elephant. These objects could be displayed along a shelf or in a corner somewhere, but a clothesline is preferable for keeping them up and out of reach. I have seen the clothesline mobile used to good effect, and recommend it to anyone

---

* I use these words with a final *x* because *x* is rarely used as an initial letter, and when it is, it usually takes a /Z/ sound. I have never seen a child confused by this.

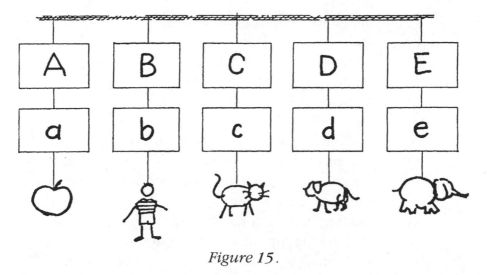

Figure 15.

who wants to spend the time to construct it. It keeps the objects both in view and out of harm's way. In ordinary circumstances, they don't get broken, mixed up, or separated from the corresponding letters. In short, a clothesline mobile is a fine idea and well worth the trouble, especially when several children are involved. The best example I have ever seen was in a second-grade classroom for high-risk youngsters—it gave the letter-sound associations a vivid reality for each child, and for the class as a whole.

3. Reading aloud

Continue reading aloud with your student (or having her read aloud to) for an average of 30 minutes each day. Make the time you spend reading together as close and as pleasant as you can. Minimize distractions, and read only when the child really wants to. (This raises an obvious exception to the rule of reading for 30 minutes per day—if the child really is not interested in having you read at a particular time, don't force her, and don't let anyone else force her. Find another time. It is highly unlikely that she will *never* want you to read aloud to her.)

Occasionally your pupil might decide that a way to get to you is to refuse to cooperate in something you want to do, like reading. If this happens, don't read. Either stop where you are until her behavior or attitude improves, or don't start at all until you're guaranteed a cooperative, attentive audience. "My reading aloud is for listening to" is a Ginott-like* argument that I've found to be logically persuasive with a variety of 2- to 5-year-olds. However you proceed, it is worth taking some pains to assure your pupil's attention.

I believe that the usual cause of inattention is disinterest in the material being read. I have no compunction about editing as I read, shortening some sections and adding emphasis in others. If you are careful to read material your student wants to hear, to keep the environment warm and supportive, and to read only when your student wants you to, you should find little difficulty gaining his attention. And as always, make it a rule to quit before the child is ready to quit. Many a child is fidgety, and has a short attention span. Aim for brief reading sessions, and stop *before* the child gets restless.

4. Things to read

Now is a splendid time to begin reading poetry together, if you have not done so already. The main benefit of reading poetry aloud is the fun of the experience, but in addition, introducing the idea of rhyme can be quite helpful in teaching a child to read. Your librarian will be able to suggest several collections of poetry that are appropriate for you and your student. Sitters, visitors, grandparents, and volunteers are often helpful in this regard as well, especially for reading a favorite poem aloud.

5. Writing & scribbling

Continue to encourage your student's writing efforts. Keep a good supply of writing materials at strategic points around the house or classroom, and urge the child to use them. Don't neglect the computer or typewriter.

---

* The late Haim Ginott, a gifted pediatrician, worked out a system for speaking with (and listening to) children. I recommend his books, which are still in print.

6. Writing together

Continue writing in your journal, or begin one if you haven't already done so. Enter what you have written on the computer, either by keyboard or by scanner, and print it out for your student. Try to use ordinary occasions to get the child involved; ask him to help you write labels, a grocery list, or a note to a friend.

7. Things to make together

Poetry and quotations scrapbook. I wish I had kept a book of poems and short quotations that my children and I have enjoyed. I didn't, but such a project might be fun for you to try. Photocopies of poems can be kept in a special folder or pasted in a scrapbook. This project is especially promising for teachers, who have easy access to copying equipment.

8. Own words

As mentioned in previous kits, your student's "own words" can include the names of friends, family members, or pets, or almost any other words that interest her. These words need not be nouns, but I suspect you will find that nouns are requested more than any other type of word. It's a good idea to print these words on index cards, which can be stored in a small filing box. Try decorating the box and labeling it "Sally's words" or something of the sort.

9. Sight words

The sight word for Kit 4 is *you*. Point it out in your reading together, talk about it, and spell it. Explain the word to your student by saying, "*y-o-u* spells [pointing to each other] *you*."

10. Games

   a. *"What letter [or sound] does __ begin with?"* In this game, the child is asked to pronounce the sound or the name of the letter that begins a word. The game is greatly enjoyed by

many children (and by this adult). It is also more challenging than the games described in Kit 3, in which the letter
sound is suggested first. Here the child is asked to *produce*
the sound.

b. *Initials.* Children are often fascinated by their initials and
those of other people. You might use people's initials in de-
signing a scrapbook page or arranging a collection of snapshots. Or you can play guessing games involving initials (e.g.,
asking, "Who is J.W.?").

c. *The letter-word challenge game.* This game begins with one
player naming a letter. The other player(s) are challenged to
state a word that begins with that letter. The player who
thinks of a word then names another letter, which the other
players have to find a word for.

    Another way of playing this game is to take turns think-
ing up words beginning with the suggested letter until you
run out of words. The last person to come up with a word
wins, and gets to suggest the next letter.

d. *Win-my-cards game.* Turn through the deck of movable alphabet cards one at a time. For each letter, the child tries to
name a word beginning with that letter. He keeps each card
for which he is able to think up a word.

    In a variation of this game, players take turns with the
cards, trying to name things beginning with each letter. You
can make it tougher, if and when you want to, by limiting
the things named to animals, toys, household items, or some
other category.

11. Mail & e-mail

If your student enjoys keeping up with correspondence, encourage her to continue corresponding with friends, relatives, politicians, and the world in general. Although you will undoubtedly be
doing most of the writing for a while, this can prove well worth the
effort. If you haven't introduced your student to e-mail, by all means

start now. The immediacy of this medium—especially when you can send e-mail to someone you know will be at a computer, and get an e-mail response right back—will be exciting for her and for you.

12. Media

Use television as a tool, as entertainment, and as an extension of experience, being careful not to overdo it. Read the TV guide together, and discuss what shows you would both like to see. When you rent movies, consider what possibilities are offered for learning. In the classroom or child care center, much use can be made of media—especially with videos and cable TV.

Review Lesson I (Kits 1-4)

After completing the first four kits, your student can be regarded as having achieved reading readiness; she has all the basic skills necessary to learn to read.

REVIEW EXERCISES

1. Go over all the letters and see if the child can still name and give a sound for each one.

2. Review the concepts covered in Kits 3 and 4. Try to make sure your pupil understands them.

3. Review your teaching by asking yourself several questions:

    a. Am I (or is somebody else) reading to the child for at least 20-30 minutes per day?

    b. Am I taking her to libraries and bookstores, or helping her locate books on the Internet or in catalogs?

    c. Are there lots of children's books around the child's house and/or classroom?

    d. Am I avoiding pressure situations?

    e. Does my student seem to enjoy the activities?

    f. Do I always make the instruction fun?

    g. Do I quit before she wants to quit?

    If you answered "no" to any of these questions, you need to address the problem area or areas. If your answer to (d) is "no," either shape up or quit the program.

UNIT II

Beginning to Read: Kits 5-9

This unit helps your student get started in learning to decode simple words. He will learn several new sight words, in addition to the concepts of rhyme and "word families." Continue to read aloud together throughout this unit.

🌱 *Kit 5: Rhymes & ending sounds*

MATERIALS

- Movable alphabet cards
- Books of children's poetry and nursery rhymes
- Pen and paper
- Computer, Web TV, word processor, or typewriter (optional)

GOALS

The main purpose of this kit is to help your student become aware of the endings of words. Since you will be focusing heavily on rhyming, it will prove helpful to read poetry and nursery rhymes together, and to play a number of rhyming games. Specific goals for this kit are as follows:

1. Learning the concept of rhyme.
2. Recognizing when one word rhymes with another.
3. Identifying "ending sounds" in words.
4. Beginning to look at written letters in words as standing for sounds.

Go on to Kit 6 when the child meets goals (2) and (3) regularly with the words listed in Section 6. At that point, it is a fair bet that he understands something of (1) and (4).

INSTRUCTIONS

1. Reading aloud

Read poems together (poems that you both like, if possible), and periodically call attention to the rhymes. Another good place to find rhymes is in songs—*stream* and *dream* in "Row, Row, Row Your Boat," for instance. The beauty of reading poetry to children is that you can keep going back to favorite poems. This is, of course, a made-to-order invitation to look for rhymes.

2. The concept of rhyming

It is easy to teach a child to identify rhymes once she understands what the term *rhyme* means. I like to begin explaining rhymes by saying that "the ends of the words sound alike," illustrating with examples—*fun-sun, silly-Billy, happy-pappy, fat-rat,* etc. At the beginning, I try to avoid talking about spelling patterns.

The easiest way to teach a child about rhyming is to rhyme some words aloud, and try playing some rhyming games. Most children will catch on without difficulty. Children often play rhyming games spontaneously. Consider "counting out" rhymes, such as "eeny meeny miney mo," or "one potato, two potato." If your pupil has trouble with the concept of rhyming, she probably hasn't been exposed to enough poetry, nursery rhymes, and songs. If that's the case, spend more time together on these activities, and encourage other adults in her life to do the same.

3. Basic rhyming games

a. *"I'm thinking of a word that rhymes with _,"* or *"I'm think- ing of something __ that rhymes with _."* You can make your hints here relatively general or specific. For instance, you may tell the child, "I'm thinking of a word that rhymes with *up*," or "I'm thinking of something you drink out of that rhymes with *up*." This game is easy and pleasant for both the child and the adult.

b. *"How many words can you think of that rhyme with _?"* You can play this game cooperatively or take turns asking and answering, whatever method suits you and the child.

c. *Rhyming pairs.* In this game, you tell the child two words, and he tells you whether or not he thinks they rhyme. For example, if you say, *"fat-cat,"* the child should respond by saying, "They rhyme." If you say, *"fat-man,"* he should re- spond, "They don't rhyme." This game is difficult, for some children more than others. Often children with ear problems will struggle here. If the child has difficulty, just make a mental note of it and go on.

4. Making rhyming words

Use the movable alphabet cards to make rhyming words. First form a word with the cards, then say that word, and ask the child to suggest a word that rhymes with it. Then form the suggested word, and move on to other rhyming words. Eventually, if possible, you should try to get your pupil to make the words.

This is a splendid game, and the more you play it, using a variety of word families, the more insight your student should have into reading. A good variation is to take turns making rhymes with the cards—you start, then you let her make one, then you make one, etc. Another variation is to type the words on your computer screen, or print them with a pencil or (preferably) a felt-tip pen, and then let your student try to write if she wants to. Yet another option is to make the words with movable plastic letters; the magnetized ones are excellent, whether used on a metal surface or not. There is an open invitation to make words with these letters—they beg to be rearranged. It is useful to get several sets of these, so that you have enough duplicates to create messages.

5. Writing

As discussed earlier, many—and perhaps most—children who read early also write (or try to write) early. You should do whatever you can to encourage any efforts at writing. Some children seem to "take" naturally to a chalkboard. Others prefer using a pencil and paper, or typing on a computer. The felt-tip pen holds a great fascination for many youngsters. Your task is to encourage your student to write in whatever way you're able.

When the child is just beginning to write, it is important not to be uptight about spelling. The research of Charles Read, Carol Chomsky, Shane Templeton, and others indicates that early-writing children follow their own spelling systems, which for them are very effective. You'll just confuse your beginning scribbler by trying to get him to spell in accordance with adult conventions or to write from left to right consistently. Before he reaches school age, most such problems will have straightened out.

6. Advanced rhyming game

In the final game in this kit, you produce rhyming words in sequence and let your pupil figure out how to pronounce them. (Use the movable alphabet cards or a felt-tip pen to build the words.)

Begin by making a base word (e.g., *man*). Read the word aloud and tell your student that you're going to make words that rhyme with it. Then, one at a time, make rhyming words (e.g., *pan, fan, tan, van,* etc.). Let her try to figure out what each word is; when she can't, tell her the word and go on. Don't make this a big production—this is a game, a logical extension of the rhyming game you played earlier. If it isn't fun, quit and play a game that *is* fun. Here are some words you may want to play with:*

bat	can	cap	bad
cat	fan	lap	dad
fat	man	tap	had
hat	pan	map	mad
mat	ran	nap	pad
pat	tan	zap	sad
rat	van		
sat			

This is just a start. You may think up many other rhyming words.

7. Pacing instruction

Please remember to play reading games only when the child wants to play. Don't wear out his interest—at the first sign of boredom or inattention, you've already played too long. Quit immediately.

* Explain or omit any unfamiliar words.

🐛 *Kit 6: Easy word families*

MATERIALS

- Movable alphabet cards
- Felt-tip pen and paper
- Children's books
- Computer, Web TV, word processor, or typewriter (optional)

GOAL

By the end of this kit your student should be able to read a few words in isolation and to recognize a few words when they are encountered in print. These goals may seem modest, but I remind you that there is plenty of time, and much is gained by starting off slow and easy. Go on to Kit 7 when your student can recognize the words on the preceding page when they are written in *families*—that is, on seeing *bad, dad,* and *had* (and hearing them read, if necessary), your student should be able to read *sad.*

INSTRUCTIONS

1. Reading aloud

Reading aloud to your student is crucial at this stage. Joint expeditions to libraries or bookstores, and/or investigation of children's Web pages, should be undertaken regularly. Talk to your pupil about your reading, and involve other adults. It seems important that several significant adults read to the child and get involved in the learning-to-read games. Grandparents, aunts, uncles, visitors, siblings, and baby-sitters are all excellent candidates to do a bit of reading to your pupil. The more she is read to, and the more interesting reading materials are in her life and the lives of those around her, the more likely it is that she will learn to read well and easily.

As you read to your pupil, be on the lookout for any of the

words in this lesson that he might be able to recognize. Some of them (e.g., *and, sat, man, can, ran, had*) are quite common, and you should come across a few of them in any reading session. Begin by pointing out one of his words on the page—most kids find this delightful. Invite him to find more, if he wants to. As you read along, from time to time (as your judgment, the story, and your pupil permit), call attention to a word he can read.

2. Games

Using the words introduced in Kit 5, continue to play rhyming games: collaborate to make rhyming words from a "base" word, or write rhymes and have your student pronounce them. Eventually, after hearing you pronounce one of the words listed in Kit 5, your student will be able to name any other word in the same family. At that point, you'll be ready to move on to Kit 7.

3. Pacing instruction

No matter how proud you may be, restrain the urge to show off your student's reading at this stage. *Never, never* have your student perform in reading for grandparents, neighbors, classmates, etc. Performance changes the relaxed, warm interaction you've built up into something else entirely. Playing nonthreatening games with you is *very* different from performing for a grandmother, or for anyone else. Performers are tense and anxious to be right, and performing for adults is often threatening for kids. This can be fatal to the learning process. This is a fine example of how writing can be useful—the child's writing can be shown or sent to grandparents and others without tension or a sense of performance, because it is a finished product.

4. Writing

Continue encouraging your student to write. Be sure that a variety of writing materials are accessible to him. Displaying them attractively increases their use in preschool classrooms, and I suspect this will occur at home as well. Write your pupil questions, and encourage him to write answers on paper or on the computer.

❦ *Kit 7: Middle sounds* a & i

MATERIALS

- Movable alphabet cards
- Felt-tip pen, and paper
- Reading books
- Computer, Web TV, typewriter, or word processor (optional)

GOAL

The goal of this kit is for your student to learn the following ideas:

1. There are often "middle sounds" in words.
2. The student knows some words whose middle sound is *a*.
3. There are other words with other middle sounds.
4. The student can read some words whose middle sound is *i*.

Go on to Kit 8 when your student can read all the words listed on the following page (Section 3).

INSTRUCTIONS

1. Reading aloud

Your student probably has favorite books or favorite passages in his books. When you read to him, be sure that he can see the print from where he's sitting. At his favorite spots, you will probably be asked to show "where it says that." Encourage this questioning. Here and there, point out the names of characters and memorable words or phrases ("Zzap!" or "Bump, bump, bump," or whatever else you think the child will find interesting).

2. Writing

As I have urged repeatedly in previous kits, you should encourage your student's writing, of any and all sorts. Again, if he does form some words, don't worry about the spelling just yet. If you can't make out what it says, have him read it to you.

3. Games

In your rhyming games (from Kit 5), begin to introduce the following word families:*

it	bill	big	in
bit	fill	dig	pin
fit	hill	fig	fin
hit	mill	pig	
lit	pill		
sit			

When you start a rhyming game, go ahead and read the first word to your student, if need be. Before going on to the next kit, play the games using these words until she knows them fairly well.

A new game to play is the "mystery word" game. Each day (or several times a day, if you like), a new word is spelled out in magnetic letters or printed on a card. Deciphering this word is worth an apple, perhaps, or a cookie—it's certainly worth a celebration.

4. Pacing instruction

Another warning is in order against the temptation to pressure the child. Below is a quick summary of don'ts:

a. *Never, never, never insist on reading aloud or playing reading games when the child is not interested.*
b. Don't continue playing any game after the child's attention begins to wander.

---

* Explain or omit any unfamiliar words.

c. Never continue playing a reading game when the child wants to quit.

d. Don't let games or reading go on for so long that your student becomes bored. Always try to quit while he's still interested.

e. Don't show off your student's reading skills—at least not yet.

🦗 *Kit 8: Beginning sounds & decoding pairs*

MATERIALS

- Movable alphabet cards
- Movable plastic letters
- Felt-tip pen and paper
- Children's books and magazines
- Computer, Web TV, word processor, or typewriter (optional)

GOAL

By the time she finishes this kit, your student should be able to discriminate between two words that differ only in their beginning sounds. Don't expect infallibility—she'll probably make mistakes—but you should stick with this kit until she understands the differences between these words. Go on to Kit 9 when your student can discriminate between the words in the pairs on the following page.

INSTRUCTIONS

1. Games

A new game begins here, as your student begins to decode pairs of words. After completing this game, your student should be fairly confident about her word discrimination skills.

Present your pupil with two words at the same time (either written words or words spelled out with the movable alphabet or plastic letters). Her task is to respond to the query *"Which of these is _____?"* or *"Show me _____."* For example, you may say to your student, "Here we have two words, *pat* and *fat* [point each one out, and talk about the differences—*pat* begins with *p* and *fat* begins with *f*, etc.]. Show me *pat*." If the child points to *pat*, say, "Okay, great! Which one says *fat*?" or "Very good—the other one says *fat*."

If the child points to the wrong word, just say, "That one says *fat*—see the *f* at the beginning?" or "That one says *fat*—the first letter is *f* for *fff*." Then ask, "Which one says *pat*?" When she answers correctly, be sure to give praise ("Fine!" or "Good for you!").

2. Reinforcements

At this stage of the program, small reinforcers are sometimes helpful, especially for the paired-word discrimination games. This adds an element of "winning," a powerful aid to motivation, at a time when you may be glad to have the help. As a reward for each correct word, you can give a raisin, a penny, an M & M, or another small token, plus a hug.

3. Paired words game

Paired words to present in this kit are as follows:*

hand-land	cat-bat	fat-pat
band-hand	cat-sat	fan-pan
sand-hand	can-pan	cap-lap
lamp-damp	in-pin	cat-rat
tap-lap	big-dig	hat-fat
tap-cap	pig-big	fat-sat
tan-man	fig-dig	bat-hat
man-pan	bit-sit	bad-dad
ran-van	fit-hit	had-bad
pad-bad	bill-mill	dad-had
mad-sad	pill-fill	dad-pad
can-ran	sit-fit	fan-tan

Use these words to help your student discriminate between the sounds at the beginnings of words. You may try other combinations as well—these words are given only as a guide. However, any pairs you make up for this kit should differ *only* in their first letter. Thus, while the combination *pan-fan* is okay for this stage of the game, *pan-pat* and *pan-pin* are too difficult. Please don't rush in-

---

* Explain or omit any unfamiliar words.

struction. For now, just concentrate on teaching the basic skills well and having fun.

❦ *Kit 9: Ending sounds & decoding more pairs*

MATERIALS

- Movable alphabet cards
- Movable plastic letters
- Felt-tip pen and paper
- Children's books
- Computer, Web TV, word processor, or typewriter (optional)

GOAL

By the time your student finishes this kit, he should be able to discriminate between two familiar words that differ only in their last letter. Go on to Review Lesson II when the child can discriminate between the paired words on the following page.

INSTRUCTIONS

1. Reading aloud

In your reading together, look for examples of familiar words and point them out to your pupil.

2. Writing

Encourage writing and other forms of word production, using the plastic letters, computer, movable alphabet, or any other means available. If you have a computer and have not yet introduced the child to it, now is a good time to do so. You'll have to explain a few differences in type (the forms of *a, t,* and *g* to which she's accustomed differ from those in typescript), but after that, your pupil should be able to do a great deal alone. Be patient, and don't expect great results at first; a certain amount of "messing around" is a useful beginning. For now it's sufficient for the child to just have the exposure to another means of producing written language. (In my own experience with two rather heavy-handed boys, it has been helpful to lay down some rules about how computers and type-writers can and cannot be used. I discourage random key punch-ing, key jamming, ribbon pulling, etc. You should do what you're comfortable with, however.)

3. Paired words game

Following the general format given in Kit 8, play the paired words game. Use the movable alphabet cards, computer, or felt-tip pen to form the paired words below. These words differ only in their last letter, so you're concentrating on "ending sounds."*

fat-fan	bad-bat	map-mat
man-map	cap-cat	cat-can
pan-pat	pad-pat	pin-pig
tap-tan	dad-dam	big-bit
sat-sad	Dad-Dan	fit-fin
rat-ran	pad-pan	fig-fin
can-cap		

* Explain or omit any unfamiliar words.

Review Lesson II (Kits 5-9)

Materials

- Movable alphabet cards
- Movable plastic letters
- Felt-tip pen and paper
- Children's books
- Computer, Web TV, word processor, or typewriter (optional)

Review

By now your student has begun reading. The words and concepts in Kits 5-9 are necessary for a young reader to master on the road to capable, mature reading. Go over these words and concepts, and play rhyming games. Review the word families introduced in Kits 5, 6, and 7, and play pair-decoding games with the word pairs from Kits 8 and 9. Read and write together as often as you can manage. Go back and read over the entries in your journal, and think about what you were doing when you wrote each entry. Look over the scrapbooks and other projects you have made. Help your student to see how written words and pictures help you to remember what has happened in the past.

UNIT III

Developing Reading Skills: Kits 10-14

This unit will help your pupil become adept at some basic reading skills. Kits 10-14 concentrate on teaching decoding of short-vowel words. Your daily reading aloud should become more of a shared experience as your student grows in reading ability.

Kit 10: More ending sounds

MATERIALS

- Movable alphabet cards
- Movable plastic letters
- Felt-tip pen and paper
- Computer, Web TV, word processor, or typewriter (optional)

GOALS

This kit will help your student learn several families of words with new ending sounds, considerably increasing the number of words she can read. Go on to Kit 11 when she can read all the words listed on the next page, and can also read them with -s added.

INSTRUCTIONS

1. Reading aloud

Continue to read aloud for at least 20 minutes a day, or make sure someone else does (30 to 40 minutes would be better, at this stage).

2. Writing

Encourage your pupil to try to write her whole name, and to write other words too, if possible. Be sure that writing materials are accessible and in working order (pencils are sharp enough, crayons are unbroken, chalk is fresh, markers are not dried out, computer is booted up, etc.). Try using a chalkboard if you haven't already. Don't forget the "magic slate"—an old technique, but lots of fun.

3. Games

Play the rhyming games used in previous kits with the following families of rhyming words:*

kick	tip	back	bag
pick	sip	tack	rag
sick	lip	jack	tag
lick	dip	pack	wag
tick	nip	rack	
wick	rip	sack	
	hip		

4. Plurals & possessives

Another step to take is to add -s to any word covered so far. To do this, first present the original word, using the movable alphabet or plastic letters, and then add an s. You can say something like this: "I'm going to add an s to *hat,* like this, and make it *hats.*" Then play around with making plurals of other words covered, or making third-person singular forms of verbs (such as *hits*) or possessives (such as *cat's*). The usual pronunciation of -s at the ends of words is s (as in *ants*), but sometimes (after g, for instance) it is pronounced z (as in *eggs*). Most children learning to read accept this—they see *bags* and read "*bagz*" without comment. Others read "*bagss...bagz.*" Still others need to be told that s at the end of a word says either s or z, depending on which one fits the way you pronounce it.

5. Sight words

Sight words for Kit 10 are *to* and *do.* Follow the teaching procedure for sight words, and review the sight words taught in previous kits.

* Explain or omit any unfamiliar words.

❦ *Kit 11: Another middle sound:* o

MATERIALS

- Movable alphabet cards
- Movable plastic letters
- Felt-tip pen and paper
- Children's books
- Computer, Web TV, word processor, or typewriter (optional)

GOALS

By the end of this kit, your student should be able to recognize several words that have *o* as the middle vowel. Go on to Kit 12 when she can recognize the words listed below, in Section 2.

INSTRUCTIONS

1. Reading aloud & writing

Continue to read aloud to your student and to encourage his writing efforts. Besides his own name, encourage him to write the names of family members, classmates, friends, pets, places, things, and so on. Increasingly, you should encourage him to use keyboards to get his writing done. This will facilitate his development of fluency in writing.

2. Rhyming games

Play the rhyming games described in Kit 5 with the following new words:*

---

* Explain or omit any unfamiliar words.

hot	hop	sock
cot	cop	dock
dot	pop	lock
lot	mop	rock
pot	sop	cock
tot	top	tick-tock
		clock*

3. Paired words game

Play the word-pair game described in Kit 8 using pairs or three-somes of words that differ only in the middle vowel. Here are some examples:**

sand-send	band-bend	land-lend
lick-lock	had-hid	pan-pin
fan-fin	sap-sip-sop	tap-tip-top
pat-pit-pot	cab-cob-cub	hip-hop
fun-fin	put-pat	cap-cop
map-mop	sit-sat	cat-cot
bat-bit	hit-hat-hot	mat-met
sack-sick-sock	fill-fell-fall	bump-jump-lump

* Note the *cl* blend beginning this word. If this poses a problem for your pupil, just skip the word.
** Explain or omit any unfamiliar words.

❦ *Kit 12: Still more middle sounds:* e & u

MATERIALS

- Movable alphabet cards
- Movable plastic letters
- Felt-tip pen and paper
- Children's books
- Computer, Web TV, word processor, or typewriter (optional)

GOAL

This kit will introduce your student to words spelled with *e* and *u* as middle sounds. By the end of this kit he should be able to read a wide range of words. Go on to Kit 13 when he can read the new words listed in Sections 2 and 3.

INSTRUCTIONS

1. Reading aloud

By now, with your help, your student may be able to read some simple books. As you read aloud with her, encourage her to read words and sentences for herself.

2. Rhyming games

Play the rhyming games described in previous kits to introduce rhyming families that use *e* and *u* as middle sounds:*

up	neck	mud	cut
cup	deck	bud	nut
	peck		

---

* Explain or omit any unfamiliar words.

jet	end	fun	duck	hen
met	bend	bun	buck	den
get	lend	sun	luck	men
let	mend	run	suck	pen
net	send	gun	tuck	ten
pet	tend	nun		
set				
vet				

3. Paired words game

As in the preceding kits, try presenting words in groups that differ only in their middle vowels:*

ran-run

net-nut-not

hat-hot-hit-hut

rock-rack

suck-sack-sick-sock

sit-sat-set

but-bit-bat-bet

pan-pin-pen

top-tip-tap

pet-pot-pat-pit**

luck-lack-lick-lock

4. Writing

Encourage your student to write, without becoming a nag. If and when he does write, he should be praised and taken seriously. Even if the result looks like hieroglyphics, take the time to figure out what the child is trying to convey and why he wrote what he did. By doing this, both of you will really learn something. Don't worry about bizarre spellings (many of them are actually quite logical when you think about them) or a tendency to reverse letters (this is common among young children, and tends to resolve itself). Also encourage use of the computer for writing.

---

* Explain or omit any unfamiliar words.
** *Put* is not pronounced as you'd expect it to be, and therefore is omitted.

❦ *Kit 13: Blending & hearing letter sounds*

MATERIALS

- Movable alphabet cards
- Movable plastic letters
- Felt-tip pen and paper
- Children's books
- Computer, Web TV, word processor, or typewriter (optional)

GOAL

By the time your student is finished with this kit, she should be able to hear and blend several consonants in her reading. Go on to Kit 14 when she can read the new words listed in Section 2.

INSTRUCTIONS

1. Reading aloud & writing

Continue reading, taking trips to libraries and bookstores, and browsing children's pages on the Web. Show your student what you are reading, and let him look there for some of his words from time to time; especially look for blends. Become "blend detectives" looking out for consonant blends everywhere—in your reading, in signs, magazines, TV, the Internet, etc. Make a big deal of it when your student finds one.

Also continue to encourage writing. If you have not already done so, see if you can get a correspondence going between your student and a distant aunt, uncle, cousin, or friend. As I suggested earlier, mail that comes directly to your student can be a powerful inducement to read and write—it brings great joy to many children. E-mail is especially useful and quick, as well as inexpensive. When it comes back to the child quickly and from far away, it is very nearly magic. Certainly it's worth a try.

2. Blending

Introduce the child to the idea of putting several letters together to make a *blend*. Here's an example: "F says *fff* and R says *rrr,* so put them together and they make *ffrrrr,* like *Fr*ank and *fr*om and *Fr*ed and *fr*iendly."

Pronounce words slowly, and then repeat them at normal speed (e.g., "a-a-n-n-d, *and,*" "b-a-a-n-n-d, *band,*" "f-f-l-l-a-a-p, *flap*"). Go over rhyming blends, then play the rhyming game with them. Point out blends in your reading (*and* is a fine one, and so is *stand*).

Enunciate blends slowly, and have your student try to guess what word you're saying. This builds awareness of the blending process.

Don't be surprised if blending proves difficult for your pupil to learn in the beginning. Just keep playing word games from previous kits, using an occasional blend from the list below. After a while, your student should begin to get the idea.

a. Write the words on this list, using felt-tip pens or movable alphabet cards, and try reading them together.

lip	lick	top	bump
slip	stick	stop	dump
flip	trick	drop	pump
clip	slick	flop	mumps
trip	flick		stump
		tap	
grump	best	trap	band
slump	nest	flap	stand
stump	pest	slap	brand
	rest	clap	grand
belt	test		
felt	vest	sing	bang
melt	crest	ring	hang
		bring	fang
pot	ant	sting	gang
spot	pant	sling	rang
	pants		sang

b. *Some more common blends.* Write the words* on this list, using felt-tip pens or movable alphabet cards, and try reading them together.

br-	cr-	gr-	pr-	tr-
bran	crab	grab	prop	trap
brag	crib	grass	prod	trill
brat	cram	gram	problem	trot
brass	crop	grin		truck
Brad	crock	grip		tramp
bring		grit(s)		
brim		grub		

* Explain or omit any unfamiliar words.

🔆 *Kit 14: More consonant blends*

MATERIALS

- Movable alphabet cards
- Movable plastic letters
- Felt-tip pen and paper
- Children's books
- Computer, Web TV, word processor, or typewriter (optional)

GOAL

By the time your student finishes this kit, he should be reasonably comfortable with consonant blends. Go on to Review Lesson III when he can read the words listed in Section 2.

INSTRUCTIONS

1. Reading aloud

Be sure you—or someone else—reads to your student for *at least* 20 minutes per day, preferably for twice that long. In your reading, give some attention to the books that have won the Newbury and Caldecott awards. These are usually first-rate, and are often much enjoyed by children. Your librarian can be a valuable resource; be sure to ask for advice on what to read. Primary-grade teachers can also be wonderfully helpful resources.

Also, remember to look for consonant blends in your reading. Continue the "blend detectives" game suggested in Kit 13, if it still amuses your student. Don't do it if it begins to be a bore or holds things up; you are the best judge.

2. Blends

a. *Paired words game.* Present the groups of words listed below,* many of which involve consonant blends. (Feel free to
think up other pairs besides these.)

ant-tan
slip-trip
flip-flap-flop
trap-slap
flat-rat
belt-felt
damp-dump
ding-dong
lamb-limb
trap-strap-strip
song-strong
best-rest-crest
send-spend
sent-spent
bell-belt-bent
flop-flap-flip
best-belt-bent
sent-tent-went
song-sang-sing
bring-ring-sing
ring-rang-rung
lamp-limp-lump
sing-sting-string
skip-slip-snip-snap-slap
lend-send-bend-mend

b. *Some more common blends.* Write the words* from the list
on the next page, using felt-tip pens or movable alphabet
cards, and try reading them together.

* Explain or omit any unfamiliar words.

cl-	*fl-*	*sl-*	*sn-*	*st-*
clam	flag	slap	snag	stop
class	flap	slip	snip	stand
clan	flat	slop	sniff	stamp
cliff	flip	sled	snug	staff
clang	fling	slit		stack
club	flop	slob	*sp-*	stem
	fluff	slot	spin	step
gl-	flex		span	stiff
glad			spit	sting
glass			spat	stick
glisten			spot	stuck
glum			spell	
			spill	

Review Lesson III (Kits 10-14)

MATERIALS

- Movable alphabet cards
- Movable plastic letters
- Felt-tip pen and paper
- Children's books
- Computer, Web TV, word processor, or typewriter (optional)

OVERVIEW

Once your student has mastered the words and concepts covered in Kits 10-14, she has begun reading. She may not be reading well, but she is certainly *able* to read selected words—a good many of them, in fact.

REVIEW

Using your movable alphabet cards or felt-tip pen, make words from the preceding kits and see if your student can read them. Make a note of which words give her trouble. Remember that young children sometimes forget things they knew quite well a few days or weeks earlier. Please don't let this bother you. Just review whatever gives your student problems and go on with your work.

When you have time, analyze the words that gave the child difficulty. Was there anything that these words had in common? What similar words could you give her to practice with? Finally, play the game again, giving attention to the areas in which your pupil needs help. *Don't hurry—there's plenty of time.*

As you read with your student, look for words and passages he can read. The book you practice on need not be a familiar one, but practicing with a familiar book will probably be more interesting for both of you, and easier for your student.

UNIT IV

Going Ahead with Reading: Kits 15-21

This unit will help your student move toward reading independently. While no attempt is made to teach every phonics rule used in English spelling, I have tried to cover the most important principles. Your ultimate goals are enjoyment and reading comprehension, which you have been building since the beginning with your reading aloud, discussions, story writing, journal keeping, and so forth. Keep these activities going as your student becomes a more fluent reader.

🌂 *Kit 15: Magic* e

MATERIALS

- Movable alphabet cards (with a new magic *e* card)
- Plastic letters
- Felt-tip pen and paper
- Children's books
- Computer, Web TV, word processor or typewriter (optional)

GOALS

This kit teaches your student how placing a silent, "magic" *e* at the end of some words makes the middle vowel become long ("say its name"). For instance, when you add the magic *e* to *tap*, it becomes *tape*. This type of change can also occur with vowels other than *a*, as in *pet-Pete, kit-kite, hop-hope, cut-cute*. Go on to Kit 16 when your student can read all the new words listed in Sections 2 and 3.

INSTRUCTIONS

1. Reading aloud

Continue to read aloud to your student. Try exploring a new field of interest—dinosaurs, mythology, Winnie the Pooh, or some other topic you haven't been reading about. Children will frequently enjoy listening to books that are quite advanced for their age, if they are sufficiently interested in the subjects or stories.

2. Magic e

Explain the idea of "magic *e*" and give some examples of its use. You might tell your student, "The magic *e* doesn't make a sound, but it makes the middle vowel say its name—that's why we call it 'magic *e*.' It changes the way we pronounce the middle letter, but the *e* itself is silent." Make a movable alphabet card for "magic *e*," using a color very different from those used for your other cards. Explain that you used a different color "just to remind you that this isn't an ordinary *e*." Demonstrate the way magic *e* works, using the following word pairs:*

tap-tape	cap-cape	kit-kite	hop-hope
van-vane	pet-Pete	pin-pine	pop-pope
mad-made	bed-bede	rid-ride	not-note
man-mane	hid-hide	spit-spite	cod-code
mat-mate	kit-kite	bit-bite	tot-tote
hat-hate	fin-fine	spin-spine	hop-hope
rat-rate	shin-shine	twin-twine	cut-cute
dam-dame	win-wine	rod-rode	dud-dude
			tub-tube

3. Rhyming games

Below is a list of word families that use magic *e*.* Use these words to play the rhyming games from Kit 5 (or, if you prefer, make up new activities).

late	bake	ride	lite	cube
date	cake	side	nite	lube
gate	fake	hide	bite	tube
hate	lake	tide	kite	
grate	make	wide		dude
plate	rake	slide	stone	Jude
slate	sake	glide	lone	nude
	take	bride	cone	rude
tale	wake		bone	
sale	snake	bike		dune
gale	stake	dike	hope	tune
male	brake	Mike	dope	prune
pale		like	nope	
Yale		trike	pope	cute
			rope	lute
				mute

* Explain or omit any unfamiliar words.

4. Writing

With your help, your pupil may be able to write fairly sophisticated prose by now; be sure to provide plenty of writing opportunities. Thank-you letters are always in order, as are letters of inquiry about subjects in which you're both interested. As I have stated before, I believe that keeping a diary or journal about the things you do together is a splendid experience for both of you. You should at least *try* to keep one. A journal can hold photographs and clippings as well, serving as a scrapbook. Any chance you get, take dictation from your student and let him read your writing back to you. Print out copies for the child to illustrate with drawings.

🦎 *Kit 16: Speech consonants & more vowel sounds*

MATERIALS

- Movable alphabet cards, including the magic *e* card
- Plastic letters
- Felt-tip pen and paper
- Children's books, newspapers, and magazines
- Computer, Web TV, word processor, or typewriter (optional)

GOAL

This kit is intended to help your student learn to associate sounds with the following letters and letter combinations:

> *ch, sh, th, wh, ph*
> *oo* as in *book*
> *oo* as in *tool*
> *-o* as in *so*
> *-o* as in *do*
> *-e* as in *me*
> *-ee* as in *bee*

Go on to Kit 17 when your student can read the new words listed in Sections 2 through 6.

INSTRUCTIONS

1. Reading aloud

Keep up your reading aloud together. With easy text, take turns reading the words. First read a few words, then stop at a word your student should be able to read, and let him read it. When you can alternate sentences, you know you're getting somewhere. Encourage your student to learn unfamiliar words by spelling them first, then "sounding them out"—saying the letter sounds slowly, and then speeding up.

2. Speech consonants

Explain to your student that there are several sounds that two letters can stand for together. These "speech consonants" are quite different from the sounds the letters make separately; they are *not* blends. The speech consonants are listed below. By this time you may find that your student already knows some or all of these.

> *sh* as in *ship*
> *ch* as in *chop*
> *th* as in *that* (hard, or voiced, *th*)
> *th* as in *with* (soft, or unvoiced, *th*)
> *wh* as in *when*

Using felt-tip pens, movable alphabet cards, plastic letters, or a computer, present the words listed below.*

a. **sh:**

ship	shut	cash	trash	wish
shush	sh!	flash	splash	fish
shack	shave	crash	fresh	slush
	shame	mash	mush	

b. **ch (*also* tch)** The *ch* and *tch* words can be lumped together or taught separately, whichever you prefer. Note that the spelling *tch* usually comes at the end of a word; *ch* is usually found at the beginning, but there are exceptions (e.g., *such* and *much*).

chop	chub	such	much
chap	chum	witch	Dutch
chip		ditch	patch

---

* Explain or omit any unfamiliar words.

c. **wh & th** (voiced and unvoiced, as in *this* and *bath*, respectively)

wh:	**voiced *th:***	**unvoiced *th:***
when	this	bath
whip	that	path
which	these	with
while	them	Beth
white	those	thick
whap!	the	thin
whack!		thump
		thud

d. **ph** (This doesn't quite belong with the rest, because in these words *ph* simply takes the sound of *f*.)

phone	telephone	elephant
Ralph	Phil	Philadelphia

3. Long e

Introduce the long *e* sound associated with *-e* and *-ee*, as in *she* and *bee*. Try the following words:*

be	fee	beet	feel
me	bee	feet	sleep
he	see	meet	sheep
she	glee	sleet	
we	whee	greet	
	flee		

4. oo

Introduce the *oo* sound, as pronounced in *too* and in these words:*
There are also two words in which just one *-o* is read like *-oo*. These
words—*do* and *to*—were learned in Kit 10 as sight words. Just ask

---

* Explain or omit any unfamiliar words.

your student to remember that *to* and *do* are different from other words. (Isn't English spelling fun?)

zoo	boo	loop	toot	room
pool	cool	tool	zoom	mushroom

5. -o *words*

Introduce the words *no, so, go,* and *ho, ho, ho.* In the long process of learning written English, your student will learn to deal with an enormous number of these exceptions and special cases, just as you did. Treat these as a matter of course, and go on. Some students find this ambiguity difficult, but most don't. If you are relaxed about spelling patterns, your student will be too. Make sure it doesn't seem like a big deal.

6. Alternate -oo *pronunciation*

The letter combination *-oo* can be pronounced either as in *too* or as in *book.* Tell this to your student and then show him the following words:*

look	book	cook	hook
rook	shook	took	

Certain words—such as *roof* and *coop*—can be pronounced either way. It is reasonably safe to say that when it comes before *k, -oo* is usually pronounced as it is in *book.* In other situations, it's usually pronounced as in *too.* The best approach in teaching this letter combination is to encourage the child to try the most common pronunciation first, and then, if that doesn't produce a recognizable word, to consider a less common pronunciation.

7. Word files

Try helping your student to list every word she knows how to read. You might even set up an index file of 3 x 5" word cards, if you are

---

* Explain or omit any unfamiliar words.

very ambitious. This is an unsurpassed way to show your student how much she is learning. But be sure to put whole word families on each card, unless you want an *enormous* file—by now the child can probably read hundreds of words.

Of course, it is easy to make a computer file of these words. This is one of the many ways in which the computer eases your work as a teacher, and facilitates the child's learning. An actual print-out of *all* the words she has learned to read can be a powerful encouragement for almost any child. This can be kept handy, added to daily, and re-printed often as it grows. It makes a *very* tangible piece of evidence of her progress as a reader.

❦ *Kit 17: Two-syllable words & two-vowel combinations*

MATERIALS

- Movable alphabet cards
- Movable plastic letters
- Felt-tip pen and paper
- Children's books, newspapers, and magazines
- Computer, Web TV, word processor, or typewriter (optional)

GOAL

This kit will introduce the child to two new instances of letter combination: (1) certain two-syllable words made by adding suffixes to words already familiar, or to other one-syllable roots; and (2) two-vowel blends and combinations that represent a variation on their sounds.

INSTRUCTIONS

1. The -ing *ending*

Introduce the *-ing* ending. Notice that final consonants often double when you add *-ing*. Point this out to your student, as you introduce the following words:

win-winning	run-running	slip-slipping	drip-dripping
sing-singing	hop-hopping	shut-shutting	shop-shopping
spin-spinning	pat-patting	hit-hitting	zip-zipping
ring-ringing	cut-cutting	do-doing	go-going
fix-fixing			

---

* Explain or omit any unfamiliar words.

2. The -y ending

Use the words in the list below to introduce the -y ending.* Explain that at the end of words, -y is pronounced quite differently from the way it is pronounced in *you*. At the end of words with two or more syllables, it is usually pronounced as in *candy*. Note that consonants sometimes double before -y.

candy	Terry	plenty	jelly
handy	Timmy	twenty	belly
puppy	Jimmy	dandy	Kelly
guppy	Billy	fancy	Tony
penny	Kenny	silly	Henry
happy	Cathy	bully	Tommy
any			

Naturally, there are exceptions. For instance, at the end of one-syllable words, such as those shown below, -y is pronounced as long *i*.

by	fly	cry	fry	sky
my	spy	dry	sly	try

Y also sounds like *i* when it is followed by a magic *e*.

bye	good-bye	lye	aye	eye

And often, *y* sounds like *i* when it follows *f* or *n*, as in these words:

defy	deny	specify

3. Comparative endings

Introduce the comparative endings -er and -est, using words from the following list:*

big-bigger-biggest	hot-hotter-hottest
fat-fatter-fattest	slick-slicker-slickest
thin-thinner-thinnest	thick-thicker-thickest

* Explain or omit any unfamiliar words.

sad-sadder-saddest   dumb-dumber-dumbest
mad-madder-maddest   fast-faster-fastest
dim-dimmer-dimmest   wet-wetter-wettest
red-redder-reddest   still-stiller-stillest

4. -es *endings*

Introduce the *-ez* sound of *-es*, as in *dishes*—this sound follows some words that end in *-s*, *-sh*, *-x*, or *-ch*.*

box-boxes   mess-messes   miss-misses
pass-passes   kiss-kisses   witch-witches
ax-axes   sash-sashes   moss-mosses
boss-bosses   wish-wishes   muss-musses
crunch-crunches   mass-masses   punch-punches
hatch-hatches   fuss-fusses   catch-catches
fox-foxes   match-matches   bus-buses
flash-flashes

5. *Reading aloud & silently*

Keep your student involved with interesting storybooks and articles. Continue reading aloud with him, and try to give him some time alone with his books. Don't force him to read on his own, but see if you can work it out—usually it works out by itself simply by making the books available and setting up the occasion. An example would be to have books available near the bed at naptime, or when the child is sick.

6. *Vowel blends*

There are a number of two-vowel and vowel-and-consonant combinations that sound like a blend of the two constituent letters. Here are some examples of words that include vowel blends. Introduce these as you think best, but without making a big deal of them.*

---

* Explain or omit any unfamiliar words.

aw:	*ou* (as in *out*):	*ou* (as in *soul*):	*ow* (as in *now*):	*ow* (as in *low*):
slaw	out	soul	bow-wow	snow
law	pout	pour	brown	slow
draw	sour		now	mow
flaw	couch		how	glow
claw	ouch	*oi:*	cow	grow
lawn	pouch	oil	pow!	show
dawn	clout	boil	town	throw
	shout	coil	gown	blow
au:		soil		bow (as in
haunt		toil		*tie a bow*)
taunt				
flaunt				
taut				
laud				
gaudy				

7. Writing

Writing is of increasing importance at this stage. You should seize any pretext to write letters. Thank public officials, or write letters to distant relatives and friends—you'll come up with plenty of reasons to write and plenty of people to write to, if you give the matter enough thought. Pen pals, notes, and even junk mail can be helpful at this stage.

Use e-mail whenever possible; junk e-mail can be particularly useful. You and your student can frame a message back to the senders of unwanted e-mail, asking them to take your name off their mailing lists. You might even let the child type the message from your draft and send it. Power!

Kit 18: More vowel combinations

MATERIALS

- Movable alphabet cards
- Movable plastic letters
- Felt-tip pen and paper
- Children's books
- Computer, Web TV, word processor, or typewriter (optional)

GOAL

This kit teaches your student various new ways of combining vowels.

INSTRUCTIONS

1. Reading aloud

Your trips to the library are more important now than ever. Continue reading aloud (the more the better), and talk about your reading—what you like best about a story, what you think will happen, etc.

2. Writing

Writing remains important, as well. Using plastic letters or a felt-tip pen and paper, try leaving messages for your student to answer. If you haven't done this yet, you might start by asking short questions that can be answered simply—with "yes," "no," or some other easy words. Then, as the practice becomes better established, you can move on to more elaborate communications. Remember not to worry about spelling! If you can't read what the child writes, have her read it to you.

3. Vowel combinations

Introduce the following vowel combinations.*

ai:	ea:		oa:
jail	beat	deal	oat
pail	neat	meal	boat
fail	heat	real	coat
nail	seat	seal	goat
hail	meat	heal	moat
mail			
rail	freak	team	groan
sail	leak	beam	
tail	peak	seam	soak
wail	streak	cream	oak
	beak		
rain		cheap	
pain	bean	heap	
lain	mean	leap	
main	lean		
vain	Jean	*but also:*	
		steak	
paid	cheap	break	
maid	heap		
laid	leap	*and:*	
raid		head	
	tea	lead	
		dead	

4. qu-

Introduce the spelling *qu-*. In English, *q* almost always appears together with *u*. It is only used alone, I believe, in words taken directly from the Arabic (such as *qaf* and *Iraqi*), which the child should not encounter often in the ordinary course of preschool reading.

---

* Explain or omit any unfamiliar words.

Thus, as a general rule, one can expect *q* to be followed by *u*. Together, these letters make the sound *kw*. Illustrate this pronunciation by introducing the following words:*

quit	quick	queen	quite	squeeze
quints	quilt	quote	quip	squint
quiz				

*Explain or omit any unfamiliar words.

🐛 *Kit 19: -r after vowels; soft c & soft g*

MATERIALS

- Movable alphabet cards
- Movable plastic letters
- Felt-tip pen and paper
- Children's books and magazines
- Computer, Web TV, word processor, or typewriter (optional)

GOAL

The goal of this kit is to help your student become familiar with several more letter-sound combinations.

INSTRUCTIONS

1. Reading aloud & writing

Continue to read aloud to your student, and keep the book-choosing and library trips fun. If reading gets to be a chore, try to figure what makes it a chore and change your approach. Continue to encourage your student to produce written material, and take turns reading aloud the passages you know she can read.

2. -er *sound*

Use the following list to introduce the sound of *-er*, as pronounced in *her.**

her	thinner	dinner	err
cutter	bigger	fatter	

Illustrate that in many words, *-ir, -ur, -urr,* and *-or* stand for the same *-er* sound.*

*Explain or omit any unfamiliar words.

sir	bird	fur	purr	tailor
fir	third	cur	burr	sailor
chirp	slur		word	

3. r *with* a & o

Demonstrate how in many words, *r* changes the sound of the *o* or *a* before it.*

a:			**o:**
art	far	farm	or
chart	car	harm	for
part	par	charm	corn
cart	jar		horn
tart	bar	card	born
dart	tar	hard	morning
mart			

4. l *or* ll *with* a & o

Before *l* or *ll*, *a* sometimes represents a slightly different sound, as in *all*, and *o* usually becomes long, as in *old*.*

all	pall	old	roll
fall	tall	gold	poll
ball	wall	mold	
gall		fold	colt
hall	Walt	hold	folk
call	malt	bold	
mall	halt		

5. Soft c

Introduce "soft" *c* and "soft" *g*. The soft sound of *c*, pronounced like *s*, is found when *c* is followed by *e*, *i*, or *y*. Examples include the following:*

*Explain or omit any unfamiliar words.

ice	dice	Cindy	cedar	cider
Tracy	cellar	cinders	pounce	decide
Cy	cent	civil	mercy	certain
cyst	twice	cigarette**	mice	cirrus
cell	once	Nancy	ace	cigar**
emergency				

6. Soft g

The "soft" sound of g, pronounced like j, is found sometimes (but not always) when g is followed by e or y. When soft g occurs in the middle of a word, it is sometimes accompanied by a d, as in *edge*. Below are several examples of words that include soft g:*

edge	page	gadget	digest	lodge
gauge	widget	suggest	pledge	gouge
budget	sludge	cage	fidget	grudge
rage	Madge	sage	dodge	budge
fudge	judge	edgy		

Here are some examples of soft g at the beginning of words:*

Gemini	geology	gelatin	Georgia	geometry
general	genuine	gem	gentle	gerbil
German	gyp	germ	gym	gesture
George	gel	gee	gentleman	geography
geranium				

(However, note the exceptions *get, gecko,* and *geek.*)

7. Before -nd

Before *-nd,* i sometimes takes the long sound, as in these words:*

find	mind	blind	hind
rind	bind	kind	wind (as in *wind a watch*)

---

* Explain or omit any unfamiliar words.

** Aside from any philosophical objections to using these words as examples, they do pair a soft c with a hard g. Omit if this presents a problem.

🌱 *Kit 20: Common sight words*

MATERIALS

- Felt-tip pen
- 3 x 5" index cards
- Computer, Web TV, word processor, or typewriter

GOAL

This kit is designed to teach your student to recognize some of the most common words, quickly and accurately.

INSTRUCTIONS

1. Word cards

Using a felt-tip pen and index cards, make a set of cards for some of the words on the sight word list (shown on the following page) that your student doesn't know yet. In printing the words on the cards, it is helpful to first draw a guideline in pencil. Or, if you like, you can print the words on the lined side of the card. Use the same simplified letter forms you used in previous kits. The letters should be about ½" high.

When your student can recognize most of the words on the first set of cards you made, begin to add a few more words from the list. Point out these words when you encounter them in your reading. Go slowly. As my son William used to say, these words are "spelled funny."

2. Games

Most of the letter games described in Kits 1 and 2 can be adapted for sight words. A few possibilities are described below.

  a. Word tree. One of the most effective activities using sight

MASTER LIST OF COMMON SIGHT WORDS

a	find	no	three
about	for	now	through
again	from	nowhere	to
all	girl	of	too
also	give	often	took
although	go	old	toy
another	good	one	two
any	good-bye	only	uncle
anyone	has	onto	under
are	have	open	underneath
as	her	ought	until
aunt	here	out	us
away	house	over	walk
baby	how	party	want
be	I	play	was
been	into	put	water
beneath	in	said	way
blue	is	say	we
boat	knot	saw	were
boy	know	see	what
brother	laugh	seen	whatever
come	little	should	when
could	look	sister	whenever
cough	may	some	where
cousin	me	something	wherever
cow	mother	that	which
day	many	the	who
do	Miss	them	why
dog	Mr.	their	will
done	Mrs.	then	with
down	Ms.	there	woman
eat	my	they	would
ever	never	this	yellow
every	nevertheless	thorough	you
father	night	though	your

words is the word tree; the child arranges the cards for sight words he can read on the wall, on a door, or in another convenient place. The more words he can read, the more cards he can place on the tree.

b. *Household object identification.* This game requires the child to tape cards with the names of household objects onto those objects—on a lamp, chair, sofa, table, light, door, etc. When the child can identify all the words, you can take the cards off the objects, mix them up (either on or off the objects), and have her restore them to their proper places.

c. *Today's word.* Another game you can play is "today's word." Each morning the child chooses a word—any word—that she wants to focus on that day. You then, with appropriate ceremony, make up a card for the word and give it to her. Every time she uses or hears the word, you should make a big deal of it. If you like, you can write these words on a calendar, one for each day.

d. *Find the word.* This game is particularly useful for very common words. You show the child a page on which a certain word can be found, and challenge him to find it. This game is appropriate for most of the words listed on the preceding page.

3. Reading aloud

As you read aloud to your student, remember to stop now and then to let her read words you know she recognizes. Often, as I suggested in Kit 19, this can be carried to the point where you take turns reading to one another.

🦗 *Kit 21: Independent reading*

MATERIALS

Word cards
Movable alphabet cards
Children's books
Computer, Web TV, word processor, or typewriter (optional)

GOAL

This kit attempts to encourage your student to read independently.

INSTRUCTIONS

Continue your reading together. Increasingly, have your student read parts of the stories to you. My caution and concern about "performing" continues to apply. I would still be slow to have the student read to others, except to you and perhaps to a much younger child (and reading to pets is always a good idea).

Keep the house or classroom full of reading materials that interest you and the child. Encourage her to talk about her reading with you and with anyone else who will listen. Continue to encourage your student to write, to use the computer, and to maintain a wide correspondence. Pen pals—and especially e-mail pen pals—are particularly helpful. Receiving e-mail notes from two or three friends or relatives each week can have a profound effect.

Have your student read with (and possibly instruct) a child who is a less expert reader. This "each one teach one" approach can work wonders. Have him use this book!

Review Lesson IV (Kits 15-21)

Kits 15-21 were designed to help your student get to the point where he can read some material by himself, and can read *parts* of most material. These kits have introduced many small details of word recognition and phonics; it is mastery of these details that will build your student's reading confidence. Now, in Part V, you will focus more on building comprehension, enjoyment, and fluency.

REVIEW EXERCISES

1. Review the words covered in Kits 15-21, forming them with the cards or plastic letters, or writing them with a felt-tip pen or on the computer. Note which words give the child difficulty, and provide more practice with similar words. Ideally, you should print out a list of *all* her words, highlighting or underlining the ones that are problematic.

2. Alternate your reading together—read a few words, then stop and let your student read a few words, and then read again. Note where the child has difficulty; work on problem areas at a later time, or tackle them immediately if the situation permits.

3. There's not much need to review your teaching here. If you've reached this point, you're bound to have been effective.

4. Award yourself a Master Teacher certificate. You've earned it!

UNIT V

Building Comprehension & Fluency: Kits 22-27

In order to become a fluent reader, your student must develop a number of comprehension skills and concepts. The comprehension skills covered in this unit are wide ranging—including, among others, understanding the facts, finding the main idea, summarizing, reading critically and analytically, inferring and synthesizing, and reading creatively. Your student actually began developing these skills long ago, as you told her stories, read aloud to her, and encouraged her to reflect on her reading abilities.

Accuracy

A commitment to accuracy is the cornerstone of good reading—the golden path to reading precisely and thoughtfully. While guessing also plays a part (especially with unknown words, foreign names, and illegible scrawls) and is addressed in this program, it is of secondary importance.

Fact

It is essential to get the facts straight. We need to be able to read for the basic knowledge of *who, what, where, when, why,* and *how*—the six essential questions of newspaper reporting. It is these facts, once grasped, that comprise the foundation upon which detailed and analytical comprehension is built.

Summary and Main Idea

Summaries and main ideas are closely related, and are usually talked about together. We ask of a new book or movie, "What was it about?" and expect a response such as, "It was about a man looking for the lost Ark," or "It was about these Harvard students who fall in love, but she dies." After identifying the main idea, we usually try to develop a more detailed description. This detail, informally arranged, constitutes a kind of summary. Summaries are not always informal, however; they can be as formal and precise as the *précis* so important to French and Swiss education, and to good schooling in many other places.

It is unfortunate that summary writing has gone out of fashion in many American schools. The ability to state what was read, clearly and succinctly, is a skill of great value. This clarity of understanding builds a foundation for critical, analytical reading, as well as for more advanced comprehension.

Critical Reading and Analysis

I use the term *critical reading* to refer to the set of skills involved in answering questions such as "Is this clear?", "Do I believe this?", or "How much of this can I believe?" I use the word *analysis* to refer to skills used to answer somewhat different questions—questions of plausibility and motivation (e.g., "Does this make logical sense?" or "Why would she help him hide the gun?"), questions of causality and sequence (e.g., "Could this have happened before that happened?"), if...then questions (e.g., "If she helped him hide the gun, then she must have known he was involved; what else did she know?"), and so on. It is critical reading and analysis that lead us to achieve to real understanding.

Inference and Synthesis

Much of what we "know" about what we read we actually infer, using outside knowledge. Consider the following sentence:

> "The fashion model wore a striking red off-the-shoulder cocktail dress with matching shoes and bag."

We assume that the woman described in this sentence also has on makeup, jewelry, stockings, lingerie, and possibly even perfume, although we do not really know, because we have not been explicitly told. From a limited set of details, we can complete the picture in our minds through inference. We do this routinely. This is important, because it is the completed pictures in our minds that we identify with, relate to, and live through vicariously. Inducing the reader to see, think, and feel with the characters is the lifeblood of fiction, biography, and drama.

Inference is what allows poets and authors to paint vivid images in readers' minds; the images a reader forms depend on her ability to bring together her knowledge of the world, her memories, her experiences and observations, and her imaginings into one coherent structure. We call this bringing together and combining a *synthesis*. Synthesis is wonderful: the new knowledge and images that are created pull everything together. Thus, while critical and analytical reading lead to real understanding, inference and synthesis make the experience yours.

Study Reading

Reading to learn is a specialized skill, one that you and your student might work on together. The skills of previewing, skimming, reading actively, and reviewing are extraordinarily useful in school and in reading for fun, and they can be learned (or at least begun) at an early age.

Imaginative Response: Reading Creatively

Imaginative reading creates, in Marianne Moore's wonderful phrase, "imaginary gardens with real toads in them." There are no unicorns, but I can read about one and see it in my mind's eye—and so can you and your pupil. Pooh, Tigger, and Eeyore are real in the imaginations of many a child (and former child). Thoreau made Walden Pond live in the minds of thousands of readers, and Sherlock Holmes, Nancy Drew, and Horatio Hornblower have friends and admirers throughout the world.

Childhood is the best time to learn to read creatively, because young children have not yet learned to suppress their imaginations. (This switching off of curiosity and imagination appears to be mostly an adult skill—I think we begin learning it seriously around junior high school, maybe earlier in some cases.)

Emotional & Physical Responses

Physiological psychologists will argue that you cannot separate the emotional response to reading from the physical response, because both are involved in any affective reaction. When reading elicits an emotion, it also brings about physical changes—whether the reader cries or becomes angry, amused, or bored. Children are often very close to their feelings, and drawing attention to how a story makes you feel is a wonderful way to begin a discussion.

Aesthetic Responses

Any time we read something that we think is lovely or well written, we are responding aesthetically. This type of response can also be negative, as when we are disgusted by the details of some crime or scandal. We respond aesthetically both to the images or ideas conveyed and to the sounds of the words themselves—especially when the words are read aloud. Keats's "Ode on a Grecian Urn" has thrilled many readers who have never actually seen an urn of the sort that he described.

Profound or Spiritual Responses

Many of us read things from time to time that move us deeply, and occasionally these texts even alter our values or the course of our lives. Many religious people, and nearly all poets, can recall reading a text that had a profound effect on them. John Keats wrote movingly of such an experience in the sonnet "Upon First Looking Into Chapman's Homer."

Fortunately, the profound response to reading is not restricted to poets or to those who are devoutly religious; it is an equal-opportunity response. A fisherman of my acquaintance reports having such an experience when reading Hemingway's "Big Two-Hearted River," a story about a young man's fishing trip on the Fox River in Michigan. A good friend and former member of Congress tells me that he is moved each time he reads the Declaration of Independence. My own first reading of Thoreau's *Walden* moved me profoundly, and subsequent readings still do.

The AA Big Book, *Alcoholics Anonymous,* has evoked a spiritual response in many a recovering alcoholic, and many people, religious and otherwise, read daily meditations to set their thoughts and feelings on a higher plane. My mother's favorite Bible verse, John 3:16, never fails to evoke deep emotion in me when I read it or hear it read. I also recall her fondness for the verses of St. Paul's Letter to the Corinthians in which he talks about love; I return to read these verses from time to time, and am unfailingly moved. I have a good many points of difference with St. Paul on other matters, but I must acknowledge that he has taught me much about love, and about myself as well. This highly personal, highly individual reaction is typical of the profound response to reading. Each of us responds to texts in our own characteristic way.

The profound or spiritual response to reading may be defined as a deeply interactive emotional, intellectual, and philosophical/aesthetic evocation within the reader, brought about by reading a specific text. It is frequently accompanied by other evidence of strong emotion, such as tears, mood shifts, and on rare occasions a profound displacement of personal values, goals, and purposes. This type of response to reading seems to incorporate most or all of the other responses discussed above. Clearly, a considerable degree of reading skill is required to be able to read a text well enough to be deeply moved by it.

❦ *Kit 22: Moving ahead with reading & writing*

MATERIALS

- Books, printouts, newspapers, and magazines
- Word lists
- Movable alphabet cards
- Plastic letters
- Writing materials
- Art supplies
- Computer, Web TV, typewriter, or word processor (optional)
- Message center or chalkboard

GOALS

In addition to continuing to read with your pupil, when using this kit you should also do the following:

1. Select readings for the two of you to share that interest your student. (If the reading ceases to interest the pupil, please stop and do something else, or find a story that is more interesting.)
2. Encourage your pupil to read independently for enjoyment and information.
3. Encourage your student to use reading and writing often in daily living, and let her see you read and write often in your daily life.
4. Talk about the things you read together and separately.
5. Keep the instruction pleasant and easy.

INSTRUCTIONS

1. What to do

a. *Begin to focus your activities around using written language—reading and writing—as a tool for living.* Redouble your efforts at correspondence with relatives and friends, using regular mail, faxes, or e-mail. Use the message center or chalkboard for frequent messages involving your student (e.g., "There is a surprise for Charles on top of my desk," or "Would you like to visit the new tiger cubs at the zoo today?").

b. *Keep a journal* together with your pupil, and make a big deal out of the daily entries. (Be sure to include snapshots and mementos like ticket stubs and programs—you'll be surprised at what a keepsake this will become.)

c. *Encourage other people to read aloud to your pupil.* Try to make sure they sit so that your student can see the print as they read, and that the reading experience is primarily recreational.

d. *As you read to the child, look for words that are of interest*—because you have encountered them before, because they are on the sight word list, or because they are unusual and may be interesting to your pupil. Call attention to these as the situation permits, but be careful not to let the process get "teachy."

e. *Talk about what you have read together.* In particular, you should seek opinions and judgments. Ask the child, "Did you like this story?" or "What did you like best about this story?" or "Who would you rather have for a friend, Pooh or Eeyore?" Remember that it's okay for the student not to like a story or something about it; encourage this kind of feedback, too. It will help you greatly in selecting reading materials, and it will help your student to develop independence of mind.

2. Things for you to make or buy

a. *Look for magazine and newspaper articles and pictures* of interest to both of you. These not only provide variety in your reading together; they also can be subjects for further exploration in encyclopedias, on the Internet, at the library, etc.

b. *Set aside a special place for your student's reading materials, journals, articles, pictures, artwork, etc.* Keep this space uncluttered and free from encroachment; this sends a strong message to your student that your work together is important. Try using a portfolio, a notebook, or a computer diskette or CD—anything that is set aside for *his own* work, and is treated with respect.

c. *Be on the lookout for mail-order opportunities.* As pointed out earlier, freebies are best. A surprising number of items are yours for the asking and will arrive through the mail, which is generally a source of great interest for a child.

d. *Watch for pictures and text on the Internet* that you can download. Be sure to get e-mail addresses so that your student can draft responses, if necessary.

3. Reading aloud & silently

a. *Find interesting materials to read together.* Use the library, book clubs, bookstores, the Internet, newspapers, magazines, and other resources. Be creative. Assuring a steady flow of good reading material is surely one of your greatest challenges as the teacher of a young child. You will probably find both your budget and your imagination stretched.

Reading aloud with a child makes the readability level (difficulty) of your materials less important, since you are present to interpret or edit anything that may be a problem. Your main concerns should be interest and enjoyment. These criteria can generally be met by choosing books on subjects that you and the child both care about. Children's literature is extraordinarily rich in variety and possibilities. Try classics like *Winnie the Pooh* and *The Wind in the Willows,* but also read contemporary books, like the recent Newbury and Caldecott award winners. Don't be afraid to use series books; Nancy Drew and the Hardy boys have delighted generations of children, and both have been updated for today's audiences.

b. *Talk over what you have read.* Most of the high-level reading skills are in fact thinking skills, skills involved in developing thoughtful responses to what has been read. These skills include identifying the facts, summarizing, finding the main idea, making inferences, engaging in critical analysis, drawing conclusions, and synthesizing what has just been learned with prior knowledge. Aesthetic and emotional responses are important, too, and can be encouraged in your discussions.

c. *Summarize your reading together.* When you finish reading aloud, try to summarize in 15 words or less what the reading was about. This can become a great game, and is in fact a formidable task—try it on the next newspaper story you read. It is a valuable basic skill in learning to think clearly about what was read. Start out generating summaries yourself, then begin forming cooperative summaries, and eventually, move your pupil toward writing summaries independently.

d. *Guide and model critical and analytical responses to your reading.* Your child's views about the reading that you do together are of considerable interest (as are yours). It is particularly important to inquire about what happened and why and how it happened, and to ask the critical question "Do you think this *could* happen?" Also important are value judgments (e.g., "Do you like this story better than the last one?"). Don't be shy about expressing your own opinions, because this shows your pupil how such conclusions are drawn.

e . *Encourage creative and artistic responses to reading*. I like the idea of drawing pictures (by hand or on a computer) for the stories you read. These don't necessarily have to be representational drawings; for instance, you can paint or draw a picture of how a story makes you feel. Another possibility is to make up your own stories, using the characters from the original plus a few of your own. You can write these stories down through dictation and preserve them as keepsakes.

f. *Facilitate your student's independent reading*. Do everything you can think of to make sure that there is a selection of things to read near her bed, and keep a steady flow of new books and other reading materials coming in. Avoid dullness and boredom.

4. *Writing together & separately*

a. *Handwriting*. Encourage your student to write stories, notes, and anything else. Remember to be tolerant of spelling idiosyncrasies, reversed or inverted letters, and transpositions (*saw* for *was,* for instance).

b. *Keyboarding*. Beginning as soon as possible, your student will very likely benefit from writing on the computer or word processor. The comparative ease of computer writing confers a powerful advantage on the student, who can easily convert his or her thoughts into print. As the cost of "speech to print" technology continues to fall, look for an even more significant empowerment of the student.

c. *Dictation and collaborative writing*. The things you write together are among the best collaborations you will ever have, at least from the standpoint of enjoyment and long-term satisfaction. Writing a story or a journal entry through dictation can be a pleasure, and it creates a valuable text for later reading together or for the child to read alone.

5. Computers

While it is entirely possible to live in this society without using computers, it is growing increasingly difficult. The day may come when
all students are required to have and use their own computers. (Indeed, that requirement is already in place in many colleges.) It makes
sense to me to start youngsters using computers at an early age, so
that they are not intimidated by the technology, and they can learn
to use it to enrich their lives and their learning. Much of the work in
these units—most notably the writing and research—can be done
with the help of computers. (It is important to note, however, that
none of these activities *requires* you to use a computer.)

6. Things to make and do together

One of the most appealing aspects of informal teaching is the great
flexibility you have to devise all manner of projects and activities
that involve written language.

    a. Journals, scrapbooks, trip diaries, and memoirs. These are
wonderful activities, and they show better than almost anything else the ability of written language to "freeze time"
and to facilitate self-examination and awareness. A journal
of a trip you take together will become a keepsake, and will
hold that trip and the associated events in perpetual store—
long after your memory of them fades. This type of writing
also allows you to revisit and, in a sense, rerun the thoughts
you had at that time: you can see where you were then, and
remember where you have come from.

    b. Birthday gifts and other presents. Almost any grandparent
will tell you that letters, cards, and homemade presents from
their grandchildren are among their most prized possessions.
Making a scrapbook filled with drawings, stories, and photographs is a creative learning project for your pupil that
gets more valuable as the years go by.

    c. Holiday observances. Holidays seem to be made for kids.

Very few children are indifferent to holidays, and all holidays have a story or stories associated with them. Holidays are full of occasions for reading and writing together. In addition to making or buying holiday cards and presents (and writing thank-you notes for the presents you receive), the two of you can do research on the holiday itself—where it came from, why we celebrate it, and how it is celebrated by children in other places.

An abundance of information is available on the Internet, as well as from print sources, about occasions as diverse as Groundhog Day, Independence Day, President's Day, Thanksgiving, Halloween, Earth Day, Kwanzaa, New Year's Day, Memorial Day, Martin Luther King Day, and Columbus Day—as well as primarily religious occasions such as Christmas, Easter, Passover, Purim, Ramadan, etc. All of these are possible topics of research for you and your student.

d. *Correspondence.* I have already talked at length about how you can use correspondence to make written language important in your student's life. Continue to encourage e-mail, letter, and fax communication with relatives. Aunts, uncles, and grandparents are excellent choices, because they are almost invariably pleased to get letters, and they are usually good about answering. If they have e-mail or a fax machine, so much the better.

Other good recipients of correspondence include politicians and public servants of all sorts. When you and your pupil write to them, they are likely to answer. This is also true of the heads of companies. (You can decide for yourself whether or not to let your student know that an administrative assistant probably drafted the letter that the senator or president signed).

As a rule, I like the idea of devoting some time every day to correspondence—a practice going back a century or more, to much less harried times. This will ensure that the daily mail's arrival becomes a special event, and children as well as adults enjoy being told by their computer that new e-mail has arrived.

e. *Field trips to points of interest.* Points of interest can include museums, nature centers, and historical, educational, or scenic places. Picnics can offer fine occasions for reading and writing: making a shopping list, reading the recipes for devilled eggs and potato salad, drawing a picture or writing an account of the event, and so on. Let your imagination guide you.

7. Vocabulary development

a. *Word list.* In some appropriate place—preferably on a computer file or diskette, or in a specially designated notebook—keep a list of words that are of interest because of their spelling patterns, their meanings, or other unique features. From time to time, review the list and add new words from your reading. Once your pupil is able to recognize a word, place a check beside it and move on to others. Encourage her to keep an up-to-date printout of the list, and try to add new words daily. This keeps the list fresh and alive. Look for names of new things, gadgets, or technology, or other new words you encounter. Also look for new words from your reading together, and add these to your list.

b. *Dictionary skills.* To improve your pupil's dictionary skills, first work with computer and electronic dictionaries, and then move on to an elementary-school edition of the print dictionary. Be sure your student sees you looking up words and using a spell-checker on a regular basis. Help him explore the adult dictionary, keeping in mind that it can be intimidating to some children (though not, I think, to most of them; many young readers *enjoy* browsing through dictionaries and encyclopedias).

c. *Games.* The more games, the merrier. You can adapt the

ones already discussed, or you can play games that are commercially available, such as Scrabble® and Lotto®. Even better, you can make up word games of your own.

One game that never fails is *Paper Chase,* in which the child locates a hidden prize by following clues—such as "Look behind the sofa," leading to (hidden behind the sofa) "Try the clock," then (in the clock) "Near the stove," then (near the stove) "In the ferns," and finally (in the ferns) the prize. This game is especially challenging when there are several possible locations for clues—several clocks, say, or several ferns.

8. Correspondence

Most children delight in getting notes and goodies through the mail. With regular mail, this process requires a bit of ongoing, timely effort. Addresses must be collected, stamps and stationery must be bought and kept on hand, a set of possible correspondents must be kept in mind, and finally, the letters must be mailed. E-mail offers much easier access—all you really need is a computer and a web service and you're in business (providing that you have or can locate the addresses of would-be correspondents).

9. Media

Electronic media—films, TV programs, radio broadcasts, audio tapes, CD's, videos, and multimedia sources—provide numerous opportunities for reading and writing. All of these can be written about, and all have written material associated with them—from TV and movie listings to CD and tape notes.

10. Searching for information

Perhaps the most important skill a child can develop is the ability to locate and learn new information (using libraries, encyclopedias, computers, the Internet, etc.). This capacity is certain to be of critical importance for life in the 21st century. None of us can possibly know everything, but we can learn how to find out what we need to know. Your most productive teaching efforts will probably be spent showing your student how to locate information that he wants or needs to access.

🌱 *Kit 23: Identifying the facts*

MATERIALS

- Books, printouts, newspapers, magazines, and word lists
- Movable alphabet cards
- Plastic letters
- Writing materials
- Art supplies
- Computer, Web TV, typewriter, or word processor (optional)
- Message center or chalkboard

GOALS

With this kit, you should continue reading together with your pupil, and continue to focus on the five basic goals outlined in Kit 22: select readings that interest your student; encourage him to read independently for enjoyment and information; let him see you read and write often in your daily life, and encourage him to do the same; talk about the things you read together and separately; and keep the instruction pleasant and easy. You should also introduce several activities that highlight the importance of understanding facts.

INSTRUCTIONS

1. What to do

There are numerous ways you can encourage your student to be aware of facts as you read together; four of these are discussed in detail below. Feel free to modify or omit any activity.

    a. Conversation. When you read together, talk about important facts as you go along. Don't teach or preach; just drop in a few comments (e.g., "So she was wearing a red dress. Do you suppose it was a really bright red, or more of a maroon or a dark red?" or "The forest must have been really scary for her.").

b. *Summaries.* After you read, summarize the important facts together. Discuss *who* the story was about, *what* happened, and *where* and *when* it happened. Also tell *how* the story ended, and, if you can figure it out, *why* it ended that way (e.g., the house fell down because it was made of straw). Some materials you read will have lots of *why* and *how* answers, and others will not. Use these questions only when they seem appropriate; omit them when they are not applicable. (Your summaries will get somewhat more sophisticated in later kits. For now, it is important to build a solid base of facts.)

c. *Finding-the-facts game.* Write the questions *Who?, What?, When?, Where?, Why?,* and *How?* on cards, and use them as you used the letter cards in the *win-my-cards game.* Keep playing games from the prior kits if your child still wants to, using key words from the stories you read (names, places, objects of importance, etc.).

d. Talk about the facts presented in any anecdote, story, or description that you hear from others or see on television. For any ball game, sitcom, game show, cartoon, or party, you can come up with answers to the questions *Who?, What?, When?, Where?, Why?,* and *How?*

   Determining how an event or story ended is not usually difficult, but your student will sometimes require help from you in determining *why* something ended as it did. Proffering suggestions and ideas of your own can be helpful, but be sure to keep the process interactive. Don't just tell the child "what happened." Say something like, "I think Roadrunner ended up getting away because he's smarter than Wile E. Coyote, and he's usually prepared for trouble. What do you think? How smart *is* Wile E. Coyote?"

   It is best to keep your interaction one of mutual problem

solving, rather than either interrogating your student or simply telling him "what the answers are." Strive for a stress-free middle ground, where you are working cooperatively to identify the facts of the story or discussion. The key concept you should try to communicate here is that facts are important, and that you two are trying to discover them.

2. Things for you to cut out, copy, or download

a. Newspaper stories are ideal for activities that focus on factual comprehension. They are usually organized around a factual base of answers to the questions *Who?*, *What?*, *When?*, *Where?*, *Why?*, and *How?* Look for brief stories in your local paper, in a national paper (e.g., *USA Today*, *The New York Times*), or in a news magazine (e.g., *TIME*, *Newsweek*).

Try to find stories that are lively, clearly written, to the point, *and* on subject matter likely to be of interest to your student. The best stories are usually those in which something happens to a clearly identified person or animal. Although there are exceptions, "place" or "'idea" stories are usually less successful at catching the interest of a child. A story about recent findings in dinosaur research might be a real attention grabber, but in general, stories about the economy, acid rain, global warming, and tax reform are unlikely to draw much enthusiasm from a 5-year-old.

b. Searching the Internet is an excellent way to find articles on topics that interest your student. The Internet also has the virtue of exciting typography. Reading material is available on a wide variety of subjects, from any number of sources. Besides the sites designated for children, you might look at encyclopedia articles, educational materials, or informational sites. You will, of course, need to screen any material you copy, since there is no way of predicting exactly what you will come across. Remember that you are looking for something short, lively, interesting, and (with your help) readable.

3. Reading aloud and silently

Emphasize pleasure reading. In your own reading and, insofar as is possible, in your child's reading, strive for literal accuracy, fluency, and factual comprehension, but be sure you don't let reading turn into schoolwork. There is a fine line here between good practice and pedantry; if you err, be sure to err on the side of informality. An error that goes uncorrected is not the end of the world; there will be another chance on another day.

a. *Reading materials.* I have already suggested befriending a librarian, teacher, or bookstore salesperson who knows a lot about children's books. It is even possible to enlist several experts for advice; this is a fine idea. Everyone's time is so limited that a committee might work out better than a single guru.

b. *Accuracy.* Accuracy is the foundation for good comprehension, but since your student is just beginning to read, be sure to avoid being critical. It is usually best to take a low-key, encouraging approach: if the child makes a mistake, simply tell him the correct word and make a mental note to review the word later. As discussed earlier, I suggest keeping a list of words that your pupil has missed and that need more attention.

c. *Fluency.* The adept reader is fluent in reading aloud (and reading silently). Although few beginning readers quickly become fluent in difficult materials, fluency in easy, familiar materials is an attainable and desirable goal. With practice, a child who reads *Hop On Pop* easily can also read it with fluency and appropriate expression.

It is helpful for you to model fluent, expressive reading for your student; this is one of the reasons why reading aloud together is so productive. The child needs to hear and see you read all sorts of material.

d. *Summary responses.* At the end of your reading sessions, talk with your student about the events that were described (e.g., "In this story Pooh went looking for honey. What else happened?"). This type of exchange helps convey the idea that narratives can be examined, remembered, and retold. Be sure to keep these discussions low-key and casual.

e. *Critical and analytical responses.* For comprehending academic texts—indeed, for comprehending most types of material—it is important to be able to read critically and analytically. Questions are always in order. Playfully done, analytical questioning (e.g., "Do you think this could really have happened?" "Can trains really talk?" "Would you like to be in Christopher Robin's place?") can add depth and range to your reading. This is the primary way we have of relating what we read to our real-world experience.

f. *Creative and artistic responses.* Perhaps the easiest, and surely one of the best ways to encourage creativity is to give your student paper and crayons, markers, or paints, and ask her to draw a picture related to what you read together. You can be quite specific (e.g., "Draw Tigger for me") or, if the mood seems right, you can leave more room for fanciful interpretation (e.g., "Draw me a picture of what it's like to be Pooh"). Future kits will explore other ways in which you can elicit the creative, artistic response to reading.

4. Reading materials

One of the biggest challenges for teachers of young readers is finding appropriate and interesting reading materials. Keep in mind the ancient teacher's maxim that "if children are interested in the subject matter, they will be able to handle greater levels of difficulty." A child who is fascinated by dinosaurs will cheerfully tackle huge words—such as *stegosaurus* or *archaeopteryx*—that intimidate the less dedicated student.

Your common sense and knowledge of your student will help greatly in selecting texts that might be of interest. For instance, the child who loves dinosaurs might also become interested in present-day reptiles; it's always worth a try. The whole process of selecting materials is characterized by this sort of trial and error, enlivened by happy accidents from time to time.

The operative concern is always to find materials that will engage your pupil's interest and curiosity. Books are always the best bet for long-term satisfaction. Favorite books and stories have long lives in our minds and imaginations. Award-winning books are always worth considering, but it is useful to remember that these awards are given by adults, not kids; if your student doesn't love this year's Caldecott Award winner, don't worry about it.

Your bookstore or library should have a list of books graded by level of difficulty. This is useful as a general guide, though it should not stop you from reading a difficult book aloud to a child, if the child is interested.

As discussed earlier, many children's magazines feature interesting stories and articles, and encyclopedias can be accessed either in print, on CD's, or on the Internet. Articles on the Internet can be downloaded and read as text, or simply read off the monitor screen (many pupils will find this easier than their teachers do, but I have misgivings about reading too much from screens).

5. Writing together and separately

    a. Handwriting. Learning to write by hand is a powerful way to assume ownership of written language—to set down your thoughts for someone else to read, or for you yourself to read sometime later. When a child writes something, she is clearly demonstrating that she can use written language as a tool to communicate and/or preserve her thoughts.

    Even if your student's writing looks like scribbling or her spelling is atrocious, continue to encourage her efforts. Ask her to read it to you; often you will see that it makes a certain amount of sense. Spelling patterns may vary, but you will find time and again that the child arrived at the spelling through some logical process. Please don't be critical of the penmanship, the spelling, or any shortcomings in spacing or neatness. You can work on those matters (which are undeniably important) *later.*

b. *Keyboarding.* The world goes forward, technology advances, and the child who can write on a computer smoothly and without hassles has great advantages—not to mention a valuable functional command of written language. Keyboarding and computer skills are well worth acquiring, and while a "hunt and peck" approach is adequate, a trained skill is priceless. I thank my own mother daily for many things she did for me, including encouraging me to learn touch-typing skills. I use these skills daily, and am grateful indeed.

A number of computer-based keyboarding programs are available through software dealers. Some are fairly straightforward, while others are more imaginative and playful. In my experience, the more game-like a program is, the better it works, but your knowledge of your own pupil's taste will be the best guide.

c. *Dictation and collaborative writing.* Some of children's best writing is done through dictation. Freed from the burden of having to write everything down, the author can soar on the wings of her own imagination. Though there are occasional exceptions, a child's dictation is typically far more fluent that whatever she might write by herself. The coming increase in availability of speech-to-print computer technology should be a great boon for children's writing.

As discussed in earlier units, a jointly kept journal will become a keepsake for both you and your student. Journals are especially valuable for recording trips and major events, and they enable the two of you to preserve an experience, to examine it at a distance, and to be "in the moment."

6. Games

As I mentioned earlier, word games like Scrabble® (or Scrabble Junior®) are great favorites with young readers. In addition, computer software stores sell a variety of computer games that involve words and reading, though some may be a good deal more complicated than you want. Shop with care.

Other games can be devised or adapted to reflect your interests and experiences. You can make the *win-my-cards game* into a word recognition and/or spelling game by writing game cards for the new words on your student's word list, or words from a list of your own. Constructing or adding to a word tree can also be useful. And as I have pointed out a number of times in earlier kits, any game you devise will probably be better than mine for your student.

7. Correspondence

Mail, of any sort, is an attention grabber for nearly all children, especially when it is addressed to them personally. A letter from grandparents, a favorite aunt, or a friend can elicit a response from your student that is difficult to duplicate with any other experience. Besides the dynamite impact of receiving the mail, there is also the challenge of framing a response and producing it—using either a computer, a fax machine, or pens and paper.

At this point in the program, I encourage you to foster correspondence as extensively as possible, drawing in far-flung relatives, friends, business associates, politicians, and others. Remember that politicians—especially those about to run for national office—usually answer children's letters. A cynic will point out that the letter from Senator Whatsis was almost certainly written by a staffer and signed by a machine, but your student doesn't necessarily know all that.

8. Media

All forms of media employ language—often written language—and all are grist for your mill. In addition, they usually involve some sort of narrative, and all of your student's comprehension skills can be fully engaged in trying to understand them.

Films and television programs are extremely useful practice vehicles for comprehension skills. You can try to answer the questions *Who?*, *What?*, *Where?*, *When?*, *Why?*, and *How?* with regard to a movie, a Saturday morning cartoon, a sitcom, or a ball game. You can also summarize the action of these media events and try to come up with main ideas. Critical and analytical skills can (and should) be brought into play; some of your most productive conversations can develop over questions of injustice when a favorite team or athlete loses, or over the believability of a commercial's incredible claims or improbable situations ("Does anybody *really* sing to a dishwasher?").

9. Searching for information

Perhaps the most attractive use of reading skills is reading to inform yourself. Kids often come to treasure the self-sufficiency of not being dependent on an adult to explain things to them. Research skills are increasingly valuable in this information age, and look to be among the most important types of preparation for life in the 21st century.

In addition to looking up information that your student expresses interest in learning, I encourage you to "manufacture" searches— either about topics that arise naturally in your discussions, or about topics that you introduce for the sole purpose of initiating an information search. These spurs to a child's essential curiosity are often remarkably productive, and can be good fun as well.

🕯 *Kit 24: Summaries & main ideas*

MATERIALS

Books, printouts, newspapers, and magazines
Word lists
Movable alphabet cards
Plastic letters
Writing materials
Art supplies
Computer, Web TV, word processor, or typewriter (optional)
Message center or chalkboard

GOAL

In this kit, you should reinforce the comprehension skills your pupil has already learned, and help him to develop new ones. Continue the basic activities described in Kit 22 (select readings that
interest your student; encourage him to read independently for enjoyment and information; let him see you read and write often in
your daily life, and encourage him to do the same; talk about the
things you read together and separately; and keep the instruction
pleasant and easy). In addition, continue the fact-focused activities
introduced in Kit 23—conversing about reading, summarizing, playing the *finding-the-facts game,* and talking about the facts involved
both in real-world events and in stories and events on TV.

INSTRUCTIONS

1. Summaries and main ideas

To develop a summary, you build on the facts. This is especially
true with narratives. Any story can be analyzed for its factual content, and the facts can be summed up in a short paragraph. One
basic principle of communication is that most narratives can be sum-

marized in five to nine sentences. Consider the story of Little Red Riding Hood:

> *Once upon a time, Red Riding Hood went walking through the Dark Forest on the way to her grandmother's house. There she found a wolf masquerading as her grandmother. After some conversation, she screamed and ran, and two woodcutters came and killed the wolf with their axes.*

This rather bloody tale can be summarized using the basic fact-finding questions discussed earlier:

Who?	Little Red Riding Hood
Where?	In the Dark Forest, and at Grandmother's house
When?	Once upon a time
What?	She escaped being eaten by a wolf
How?	By screaming and running

(The question of *why* is somewhat difficult to answer; many different responses are possible.)

If pressed to come up with a main idea for this story, you might consider several possibilities:

a. This wolf was untrustworthy.
b. The world is dangerous: be careful.
c. Red Riding Hood escaped by screaming and running; or
d. The wolf got what he deserved.

I know of no precise formula for deriving the main idea, but as a rule, the broadest principle is usually appropriate. Main ideas can often be found in the title or subtitle, if there are any; if there are not, try looking to the "moral" of the story. Ask the question, "What does it mean?" This approach usually works fairly well with narratives, and even with stories of specific events. For example, in the account of a basketball game in which the home team upset a highly favored opponent, the main idea—the moral of the tale—might be

that "teamwork, good coaching, and strong motivation can sometimes triumph over superior ability."

2. Things for you to cut out, download, or buy

Look for newspaper, Internet, and magazine articles that are straightforward and likely to interest your student. Most of these will probably be narratives—accounts of an event or events that took place
at a stated time and place. Others might be expository articles on
topics of interest. In addition to dinosaurs, which I mentioned earlier, such topics as Barbie collecting, pets, and wild animals can
also make for lively reading. Enjoy.

🦟 *Kit 25: Critical & analytical reading*

MATERIALS

- Books, printouts, newspapers, and magazines
- Word lists
- Movable alphabet cards
- Plastic letters
- Writing materials
- Art supplies
- Computer, Web TV, word processor, or typewriter (optional)
- Message center or chalkboard

GOAL

In this kit, you should continue the activities introduced in Kits 22, 23, and 24, and begin to focus on critical and analytical reading skills.

INSTRUCTIONS

1. Critical and analytical reading skills

As discussed earlier, in order to develop a summary, a reader builds on the facts. Once the summary is clear, the main idea is formulated, and the reader is in a position to think critically. Several questions arise:

- *Do I believe this?*
- *Does this make sense? Is it logical?*
- *Does it fit with things I already know?*
- *How do I know whether it is true or untrue?*
- *Will other people believe this? Who?*
- *What are the author's biases? Is he or she trying to sell me something?*

- *What assumptions is the author making?*
- *Is there something the author is not saying? Has anything been left out of the story?*
- *Would I tell the story differently?*

You and your student can easily make up questions of your own that get at the essence of a story's credibility. Readers are often too credulous; remind your student that not everything she reads will be true, and that few things she reads will be unbiased. One of the most important skills for a reader growing to maturity in the 21st century is a critical and thoughtful approach to information.

2. Things for you to cut out, download, or buy

Begin analyzing the viewpoints expressed in the newspaper, Internet, and magazine articles you read. In particular, you should look out for advertisements, editorials, and other examples of writing meant to persuade the reader. Practice critiquing these with your student, summarizing and restating each argument and deciding which parts of it you can agree with.

🦋 Kit 26: Creative & inferential responses to reading

MATERIALS

- Books, printouts, newspapers, and magazines
- Word lists
- Movable alphabet cards
- Plastic letters
- Writing materials
- Art supplies
- Computer, Web TV, word processor, or typewriter (optional)
- Message center or chalkboard

GOAL

The basic goal of this kit—in addition to reinforcing skills already learned—is for you and your pupil to work on developing two new aspects of comprehension: creative and inferential responses to reading. Continue to focus on the five basic goals outlined in Kit 22 and the standing assignments from Kits 23 through 25 (identifying facts, developing summaries and main ideas, and reading critically and analytically), and introduce the new activities discussed below.

INSTRUCTIONS

1. Creative and inferential reading skills

Mature readers read with their imaginations. As they process the descriptions written by an author, vivid images are created in their minds. This creative process is often described as "reading between the lines," "getting the big picture," or "filling in the outlines"; teachers commonly refer to it as "going beyond the text."

As listeners, we routinely "fill in the blanks." For instance, when someone tells you about a wedding and mentions that the bride wore a lovely white dress, you probably assume that the groom and best man were also appropriately dressed, even if you are not explicitly told that information. If you are told that the bride threw her bouquet and that it was caught by one of her bridesmaids, you can probably imagine the scene fairly clearly, although many of the details must be supplied by your imagination.

In ordinary practice, we create or recreate much information to fill in details of descriptions of events and situations. Take Robert Frost's classic poem *Stopping by Woods on a Snowy Evening*. Read it to yourself, perhaps twice, and concentrate on producing a vivid image of the scene and of the narrator.

Stopping by Woods on a Snowy Evening

Whose woods these are I think I know,
His house is in the village though;
He will not see me stopping here
To watch his woods fill up with snow.

My little horse must think it queer
To stop without a farmhouse near
Between the woods and frozen lake
The darkest evening of the year.

He gives his harness bells a shake
To ask if there is some mistake.
The only other sound's the sweep
Of easy wind and downy flake.

The woods are lovely, dark and deep,
But I have promises to keep,
And miles to go before I sleep,
And miles to go before I sleep.

While those words of the poem supply the basis for our under-standing, we fill in many of the details with our imaginations and background knowledge. For example, it is common to assume that the scene takes place in New England, because that is where Frost lived for much of his life. Nothing in the poem, however, clearly indicates any specific location. Similarly, although the speaker in the poem is commonly assumed to be male, probably because Frost was male, nothing in the poem tells us so. (We know the gender of the horse from the line "He gives his harness bells a shake," and we know the gender of the owner from the line "He will not see me stopping here...") We also don't know when this scene took place, but it is usually surmised to have occurred quite a few years ago, when such transportation was common. Upon further analysis of the poem, many more such details will occur to you.

Together with your pupil, open up a discussion about this poem. First, read the poem aloud and talk about it as you usually talk about the things you read together. Note the inferences your student makes, and consider how she came to make them. Resist the temptation to tell her what is going on or what she should be think-ing. If she doesn't know much about Robert Frost, she may con-clude that the speaker is a Canadian midwife, a Swiss ski instructor, or a kindergarten teacher. Your task in this exercise is to listen to her and try to understand how she thinks about reading.

Extend your focus on inference into your reading of newspa-per, Internet, and magazine articles. After summarizing the narra-tives and stating the main ideas or themes, develop answers to in-terpretive questions such as the following:

- *What happens next?*
- *And then what happens?*
- *How are the characters dressed?*
- *How do they feel?*
- *What do they say to one another?*

Think of other questions you and your student might raise about "the story after the story," and about what happened before the story began. Also consider how the story might have turned out differently, and ask any other "what if" questions that come to mind.

Good readers tend to be creative readers. The process of reading creatively is a long one, beginning early and lasting over a lifetime. Practice and encouragement can surely help, especially if done with enthusiasm and enjoyment.

🦋 Kit 27: Helping a child become a lifelong reader

MATERIALS

- Books, printouts, newspapers, and magazines
- Word lists
- Movable alphabet cards
- Plastic letters
- Writing materials
- Art supplies
- Computer, Web TV, word processor, or typewriter (optional)
- Message center or chalkboard

GOAL

The main goal of this kit is for you and your pupil to develop a list of materials you want to read for pleasure. In addition, with the activities begun in Kits 22 through 26, you should continue working to extend your pupil's skills in fact identification, summarizing, and critical, creative, and inferential responses to reading.

PREPARING FOR A LIFETIME OF READING

In my view, there are three essential components to becoming a lifelong reader: enjoyment, skill, and opportunity.

Enjoyment, in my view, is the most important factor. People who don't enjoy reading are rarely inclined to choose reading for pleasure over the many other available forms of activity; without the element of pleasure, the would-be reader is more likely to become a televiewer or a computer wizard instead. The enjoyment of reading begins very early in childhood, with the joys of being read aloud to, of holding picture books, of talking about stories and hearing them told, and of early efforts at writing and correspondence. It is because of the powerful influence of enjoyment that I and other teachers of young children are so concerned with keeping the reading process fun.

The second factor in becoming a lifelong reader is skill. All of us tend to do for fun those things we do well, and it follows that an adept reader is more likely to read for pleasure than one who reads poorly and with great effort. Teaching children the rudiments of reading, writing, and comprehension skills confers on them a great blessing; it is a gift that truly goes on giving, throughout their lifetimes.

The final factor in becoming a lifelong reader is opportunity. As the Bible reminds us, "as the twig is bent, so grows the tree..." It makes sense for us to start young children off as readers, to flood their environment with written language. Offer your student a wealth of books, magazines, and printouts, as well as opportunities to read them. Let him see you using written language meaningfully in your life. Continue to bring books and print into your interactions, and to make reading and writing an important part of your relationship. This should be sufficient, and if all goes well, you will be able to look back years from now and take deep pleasure in having given the singular and priceless gift of reading.

Afterword

Now that you have worked your way through the kits and the ideas involved, you and your pupil are ready to continue the great adventure of lifelong reading.

As we have often discussed in our work together in the kits, having your student see *you* read is far and away the best lesson you can teach, and is much more persuasive than any lecture you could deliver. The more you read, and the more your student sees that reading is meaningful and important in your life, the more it is likely to become meaningful and important in your student's life.

As a way of keeping this interaction current, I like the idea of following a particular ongoing feature in the newspaper, or a magazine that you both read, and that you can discuss whenever you get together. Good examples might be the ongoing fortunes of a sports team or teams, a favorite columnist, film reviews, or an international story. (I will readily concede that perhaps few young children are eager to follow, for example, the quest for peace in the Middle East—but there are some who will.) Seek out an ongoing interest that will require you both to read, and pursue it together.

Another important way is to continue to read together, books as well as short stories, essays, and poetry. Books that are forbiddingly difficult for younger children, such as *Tom Sawyer* or *The House of the Seven Gables,* become an adventure when read aloud together over a period of time. Dickens and Cooper are magnificent to read aloud, when you have the leisure (and are there in person) to explain the hard or unfamiliar words, and P.G. Wodehouse is as funny when read aloud as he is when dramatized on PBS. But not only literary gems are good to read—news magazines and items from the Internet, as well as daily and Sunday news stories, make wonderful reading. One of the best things about reading from the daily paper (or better, the Sunday paper) is that it helps your student get used to the more leisurely and in-depth reportage of the print media.

Television news has us all retrained, conditioned to take our news in sound bites, and while that may be an inescapable part of living in the 20th and 21st centuries, we can from time to time usefully cultivate a more traditional approach. Those of us who have been around a while can remember the days when people read aloud to each other in the evenings for pleasure, as a family activity. While I am not much of a social critic, it seems to me that much would be gained by reinstating this mostly-vanished pursuit. Certainly children's reading and language skills—especially their expressiveness and vocabularies—would be thereby enhanced.

Finally, providing things to read is always a productive task for a teacher to take on, especially when the pupil has been successful, hard-working and devoted. Quality of reading matter is important here, but quantity is significant as well. I can remember with what glee I devoured a great stack of outdoor magazines on hunting and fishing as a boy, as well as a long shelf full of old *National Geographics* and, best of all, several years of back issues of *Reader's Digest.* Judged on literary merit exclusively, these were admittedly not all that great, but on the basis of general information and interest, they were wonderful, and they fed and developed a wide-ranging curiosity that has stayed with me throughout a varied and busy professional life. That curiosity is one of my most prized possessions.

Holidays, especially birthdays, are great occasions for gifts of books and especially subscriptions to magazines. I encourage you to give readable gifts, as well as to suggest these to parents, grandparents, godparents, aunts and uncles and others who might be considering giving your pupil a present. The more books the better, it seems to me. I was extraordinarily lucky in this regard: my parents were newspaper people, and got lots of books which they brought home and let me read. (I occasionally got to help my parents write the review of a children's book, which I thought was a great treat.)

Books and magazines are by no means the only print medium. Now that your student is literate, the two of you can engage in e-mail or other correspondence, forwarding clippings and photos of items of interest that you can subsequently discuss, either in person or by correspondence. Pamphlets and articles are also readily available; be on the lookout for anything in print that might interest your now-reading student.

I particularly like the gift of CD-ROMs, software, and other ways of putting print and graphic technology on the computer screen. One abiding and welcome interest on the part of any teacher helping students become lifelong readers can be to help build their students' reference libraries. In this regard, books like a thesaurus, a *Field Guide to the North American Birds, The Atlas of the Stars and Planets,* or an annotated scholar's Bible are wonderful gifts that keep on giving, and are likely to keep an honored place in the student's library for many years to come. These reference texts are now available in both print and electronic versions, and I encourage you to seek them out. Think of the long-term value of the book or CD in the child's library. An encyclopedia of classic cars or historic military weapons, for example, or a reference work on dinosaurs, will have a long shelf life, and will be useful on many occasions during the student's academic career.

We discussed earlier the great advantages that lie in reading a *series* of books—that great marketing device of many a publisher in the last two centuries. It is said that impatient enthusiasts lined up at the docks waiting for the ships coming from England, bearing the latest installments of Dickens' serials. And I can certainly remember myself as a kid waiting eagerly for the arrival of *The Saturday Evening Post* and its latest serial story; I read them eagerly, though they always left me hanging. My mother wrote newspaper serials, which seems to be a vanished art form these days, but it was one I remember with pleasure. (I will admit that I rarely told any of my macho friends that I actually read the newspaper serials, which were seen as women's fare.)

Reading together and thereby getting your student hooked into a series of books that has many more volumes is somewhat controlling, but it also does him a great favor. You and he can go on to read all the *Hornblower* or *Sherlock Holmes* or *Nancy Drew* or *Hardy Boys* stories together, or you can leave them for some future reading. Either way, it will be a lasting gift.

Finally, reading together after your student has become able to read for herself is a deeply satisfying and interactive pursuit, as well as one that can give you both great pleasure. You will be able to tackle books together that you might not be able or willing to read to her alone. I remember enjoying Charles and Mary Lamb's *Tales From Shakespeare*, taking turns reading with my mother, to both of our delight. Besides being hugely entertaining, it left me with a lifetime fondness for Shakespeare, which is surely a good thing for a teacher to have.

I salute you on the rest of your journey with your pupil. You have both come a very long way, and you have surely accomplished great things. You have given your pupil something that no one can ever take away, and you have deeply enriched all her days with a skill that will prove greatly useful in more ways than can be listed. Best of all, you two have come to understand each other in that special way that teachers and their students have, and that is wonderful indeed.

I wish you lives filled with happy reading, and extend my congratulations to you both.

ABOUT THE AUTHOR

Wood Smethurst, Ed.D., is the co-founder and headmaster of the innovative Ben Franklin Academy in Atlanta, Georgia. He was also one of the founders of two other innovative Atlanta schools, Paideia and the Galloway School. He was previously the director of Emory University's Reading Center and Catch-Up School. He is the co-author (with William R. Luckie) of *Study Power: Study Skills to Enhance Your Learning and Your Grades* (Brookline Books, 1997), as well as other professional books and articles. He has taught for 37 years in public and private schools and universities.

REFERENCES

Chall, J.S. (1967). *Learning to read: The great debate* (updated ed.: 1983). New York: McGraw-Hill.

Chall, J.S. (1983). *Stages of reading development* (2nd ed.: 1996). New York: Harcourt Brace.

Durkin, D. (1966). *Children who read early.* New York: Columbia Teachers College Press.

Durkin, D. (1974). *Teaching them to read.* New York: Allyn & Bacon.

Durrell, D. (1956). *Improving reading instruction.* Tarrytown, NY: World Books.

Durrell, D. (1958). First grade reading success study: A summary. *Journal of Education, 140,* 1-6.

Manguel, A. (1996). *A history of reading.* New York: Viking.

Smethurst, W. (1975). *Teaching young children to read at home.* New York: McGraw-Hill.

Smethurst, W. (1987). *Early beginnings, success, and failure in teaching young children to read: Some abiding questions and intriguing possibilities.* (ERIC Document Reproduction Service No. ED 279 698)